PYTHON PROGRAMMING FOR BEGINNERS

THE MOST UPDATED BIBLE TO MASTER PYTHON FROM SCRATCH IN LESS THAN 7 MINUTES A DAY | LEARN HOW TO PROGRAM WITH HANDS-ON EXERCISES

LEONARD J. LEDGER

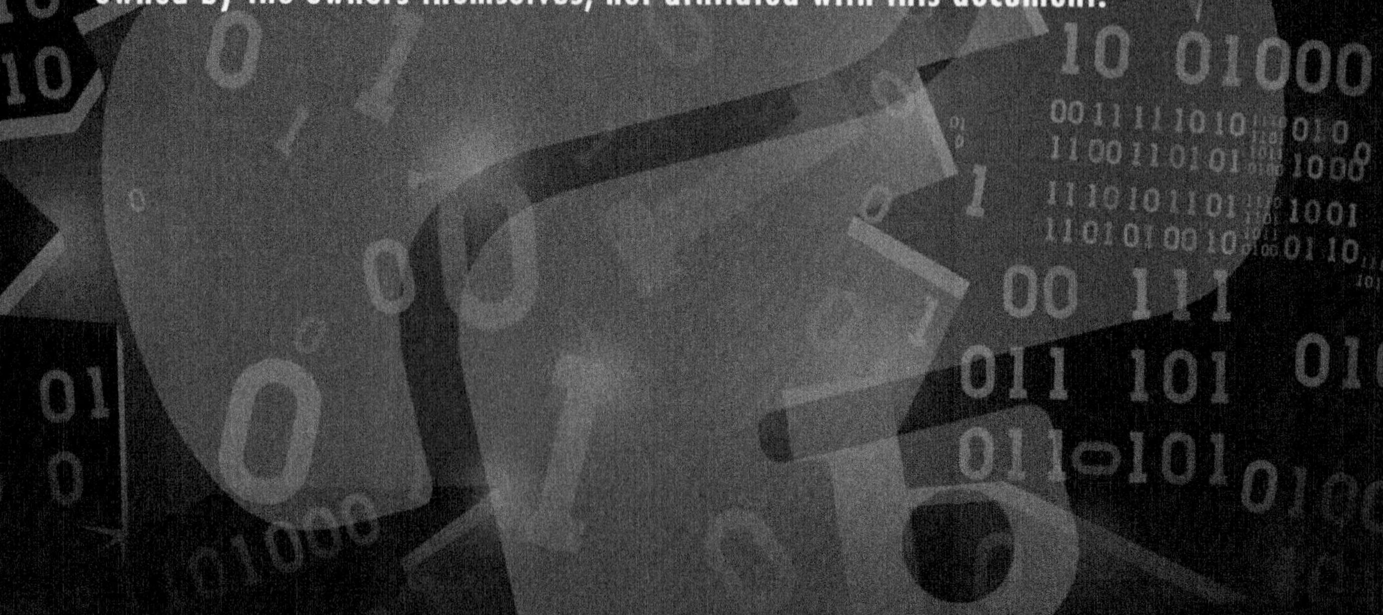

TABLE OF CONTENTS

Introduction

Thank you very much for getting your hands on this book! This book is written to help you learn Python programming swiftly, whether you are an established computer programmer or a total novice. Topics have been carefully chosen to provide you with a detailed introduction to Python while avoiding knowledge overload, but before we get started on this exciting journey, let's answer a basic question:

Best way to read this book?

When it comes to reading technical books, there is no right or wrong way. It is on the reader how they want to progress. This book has both written and embedded code examples with output which will help understand the working of Python code. Whenever a new programming concept starts, it starts with explaining its syntax and then works its way from there. In this book, the fundamentals of programming are described in detail.

Chapter 1: Introduction To Python

1.1. History of Programming Language

Programming language is, without a doubt, the essential unit used in the modern technological World. It is believed to be the collection of orders and instructions that we provide to the machines in order for them to conduct a specific task. For instance, if you offer some instructions to add two numbers, the computer will do it for you and tell you the proper answer, depending on your instructions. There are two important categories of programming languages:

- Basic Programming Languages
- Advanced Programming Languages

Low-level languages are programming languages that contain the most fundamental instructions a computer can comprehend. In contrast to the high-level languages used by software developers, low-level code is frequently incomprehensible to humans. Low-level programming languages include assembly language and machine language. High-level languages, such as C#, C++, and Python, are used to construct software applications and scripts. Using an IDE or a text editor, a programmer can develop and edit source code for high-level programming languages. However, a computer cannot recognize high-level language code, so high-level languages are translated into machine code (low-level language).

Compared to high-level languages, assembly language is closer to the computer's comprehension. It consists of command phrases such as ADD (add), SUB (subtract), and MOV (move) (move). These commands execute fundamental operations, such as reading and writing memory register values and doing calculations. Even though assembly language is considered a low-level programming language, it must nevertheless be translated into machine code for computers to comprehend it. For this conversion, Assembler is used.

High-level languages are designed for programmers and developers to create programs without understanding machine code. Each high-level language has its own set of rules and syntax.

On the other hand, the history of the development of programming languages is extensive and varied. There are about 700+ programming languages used in computer science, each with its distinct syntax and set of capabilities. It is common knowledge that Charles Babbage was the inventor of the computer, but it is less well known that he was not the first person to write computer code. Ada Lovalace is credited with developing the first ever computer programming language in the year 1883. Assembly language, a form of computer programming language, was initially used for the first time in 1949. And it was in the late 1980s that Guido Van Rossum created a powerful language that is procedural, object-oriented, and functional, known as Python.

1.2. What Is Python?

Monty Python, a comedy group, is the inspiration for the name of this language. The language is being used in a wide variety of application fields. These include applications for education and scientific research, as well as software development and web development. Desktop GUI development is also included. Therefore, it encompasses a sizable portion of practically all aspects of development. Its ease of use and reliability are the primary contributors to its widespread acceptance, although there are many additional reasons.

The language prioritizes code readability and simplicity to let developers create software quickly. Python code, like the code of other high-level programming languages, is similar to the English language, which machines cannot understand. Before we can write, evaluate, and run our Python programs, we need to install a specialized Programme called the Python interpreter, which is responsible for deciphering the Python code we write.

Third-party tools like Py2exe and Pyinstaller make it possible to turn our Python code into self-contained executables for Windows and Mac OS, two of the most popular computer operating systems. Because of this, we can freely share our Python applications with everyone, regardless of whether they have Python installed.

1.3. Why Use Python?

A vast selection of high-level programming languages accessible today, including C, C++, and Java, amongst others. The encouraging news is that all high-level programming languages are highly derivative of one another. The syntax, the available libraries, and the ways we access those libraries are the primary aspects that are different. When we develop our computer programs, we can use a library, which is nothing more than a collection of resources and codes that have already been written. If you master one language, you will be able to pick up another language quickly and simply in a far shorter amount of time than it took you to master the first language.

Python is an excellent language for those just beginning their programming careers. Python's ease of use is one of its most notable characteristics, and this quality makes it the perfect programming language for novices to grasp. Compared to languages such as C, most tasks that may be accomplished by programs written in Python require a far lower number of lines of code, which results in fewer programming errors and a reduction in the amount of time required for the development. In addition, Python comes with a sizable library of third-party resources, which can be used to expand the language's capabilities. As a result of this, Python may be utilized for a wide range of purposes, including the construction of desktop applications, database applications, network programming, game programming, and even mobile application development. Python is a cross-platform programming language, implying that code developed for one operating system, such as Windows, will run well on other operating systems, such as macOS or Linux, without needing to modify the Python source code.

1.4. Distinctive Features of Python

Python's numerous helpful features set it apart as a worthwhile programming language. Dynamic memory allocation and support for both object-oriented and procedural programming styles are also included. We've outlined some key specs down below.

1. Intuitive and simple to use:

Python is a simple language to pick up if you're interested in learning to code. Its syntax is easy to learn and very close to that of English. The indentation of a code block, rather than a semicolon or curly bracket, is something that separates it from the surrounding code. Those just starting to make their way out in computer programming should start with this language.

2. Interpreted Language:

Since Python is interpreted, its code is run line by line. The fact that it is an interpreted language has the benefit of being both portable and simple to debug.

3. Verbal Expression:

You only need a few lines of code with Python to accomplish complex tasks. As an example, consider the classic "hello world" program: ("Hello World"). In contrast to languages like Java or C, which require numerous lines to execute, this will only take one.

4. Open Source and Free:

Python can be downloaded and used by anyone for no cost. You can download it for nothing at www.python.org. A sizable global community actively develops new Python libraries, scripts, and tools. The Python community welcomes contributions from everyone. Its source code is freely available to the public, hence the term "open-source."

5. Language Portability:

Python is cross-platform and works just as well on Windows, Linux, UNIX, Mac OS X, etc. We can therefore conclude that Python is a highly portable language. It allows developers to create software for multiple platforms at once with only a single code base.

6. An Object-oriented Language:

Python is an object-oriented language; therefore, it allows for developing notions like classes and objects. It allows for several object-oriented features like inheritance, polymorphism, encapsulation, etc. A less amount of code can be written for more complex applications using the object-oriented approach.

7. Substantial Standard Library:

It offers a plethora of libraries for use in areas such as web development, machine learning, and scripting. Several machine learning libraries are available, including Tensor flow, Pandas, NumPy, Keras, Pytorch, etc. Python's most popular web development frameworks are Flask and Django.

Versatile:

Versatility means that our Python code can be compiled in other languages like C or C++ and used in various ways. The code is compiled down to "byte code," which may then be executed on any platform.

8. Coordinated:

It's easy to use with other languages like C, C++, Java, etc. In the same way, as C, C++, and Java execute code sequentially, Python does. It helps in the facilitation of the process of debugging the program.

9. GUI support:

Desktop applications nowadays are typically built with a graphical user interface. The libraries PyQT5, Tkinter, and Kivy are utilized during the web application development process.

10. Dynamic Memory Allocation (DMA):

The data type of a variable is optional in Python. When we assign a value to the variable, the RAM is allocated to it at runtime. Assuming x has the integer value 550, we may omit the assignment int x = 550 from our code. You can simply record x = 550 in your records as a string

11. Incorporable:

Python code can incorporate the other language's source code. Aside from Python, we may also use other programming languages' source code. It allows us to incorporate code from other languages.

Chapter 2: Preparing for Python

2.1. Setting Up Python

As the Python website says, "Python 2.x is history, and Python 3.x is the language's present and future." In fact, Python 3 will be used in this book. Also, "Python 3 gets rid of many quirks that can trip up new programmers without reason." But keep in mind that Python 2 is still used quite a bit. About 90% of Python 2 and Python 3 are the same. So, if you learn Python 3, you should be able to understand code written in Python 2 with little trouble.

The first thing you need to do if you want to become a Python developer is to install or update Python on your PC. You can begin the setup and installation process in several different ways, including downloading official Python distributions from Python.org, installing from a package manager (Anaconda), or installing specialized distributions for scientific computing, the Internet of Things, and embedded systems.

We will use the simplest method to install and set up Python in the most popular operating systems.

2.2: Steps to Install Python

- **Windows**

  (*Given below are steps to download Python on windows*)

Step 1: Open your browser and go to Python's official website's download page (https://www.python.org/downloads/)

Step 2: Choose the most recent Python version to download and install.

Python's Windows download page provides the most recent and secure releases. There are different installers for the 32-bit (x86) and 64-bit (x86-64) versions of Windows. When authoring this book, the latest version of Python is 3.10.6 (this might be different in your case).

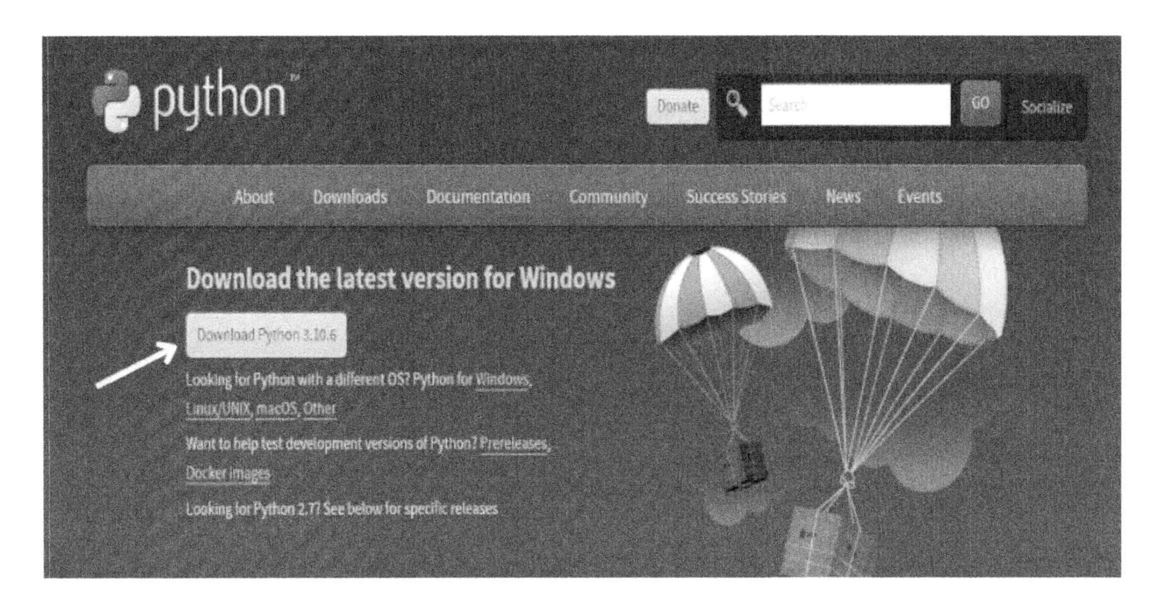

Press the yellow download button, and the browser will start downloading the python installer.

(*Given below are steps to install Python on windows*)

Step 3: Go to your downloads folder and double-click on the recently downloaded python installer. This will open up the setup wizard.

Step 4: There are two ways provided by the setup wizard: customized installation or the install now button

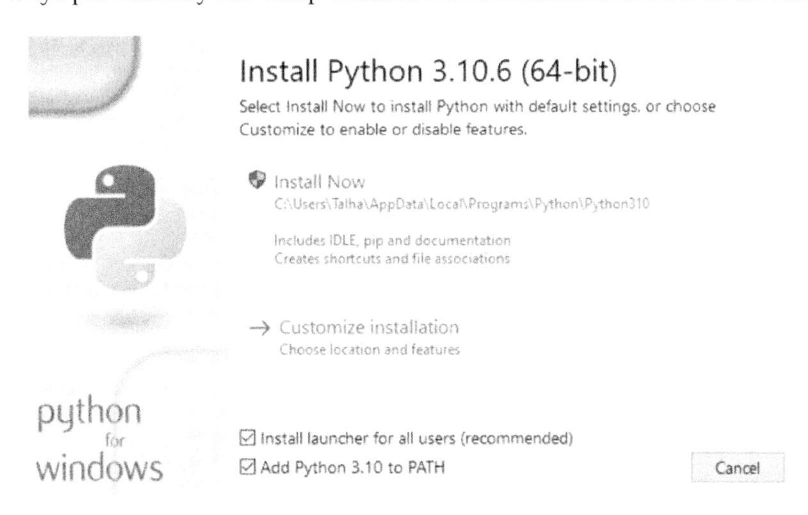

Make sure to tick the 'Add Python to Path' checkbox.

Step 5: Choose the "Install Now" option as this is recommended for beginners and includes all of the tools; this may open up a popup depending on your windows setting.

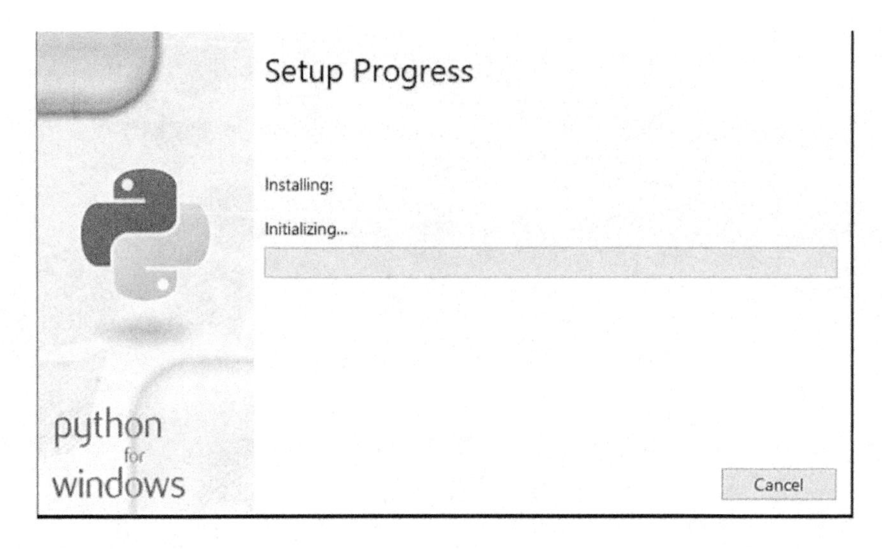

Step 6: After the installation is complete, a new window will open in the installer; click the close button.

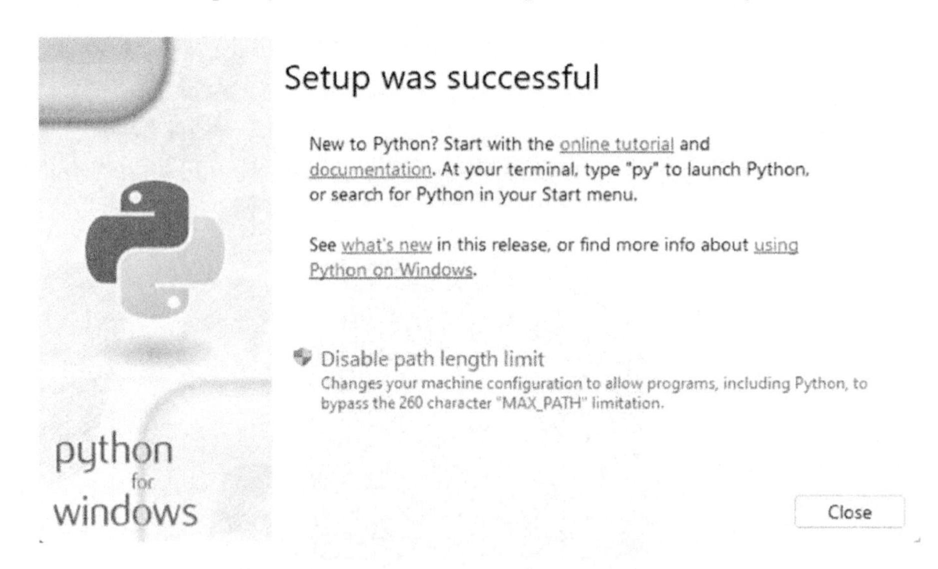

To verify your installation, open the start button and type CMD to view the command prompt.

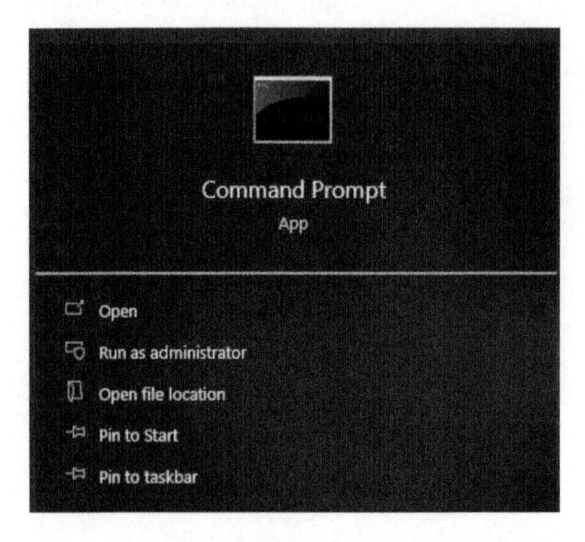

Click open, and this will open up the CMD window; now enter the following command in CMD:

Python –version

```
Command Prompt
Microsoft Windows [Version 10.0.19044.1826]
(c) Microsoft Corporation. All rights reserved.

C:\Users\Talha>python --version
Python 3.10.6
```

It confirms that Python has been installed successfully on your windows machine!

- macOS

  (*Given below are steps to download Python on macOS*)

Python on a Mac running macOS is identical to Python on any Unix platform. Still, several special features are worth mentioning, such as the Integrated Development Environment (IDE) and the Package Manager. Python's official website (https://www.python.org) hosts the latest version of Python 3, which you may download and install right now. You can get the latest "universal binary" version of Python, which works seamlessly on the Mac's new Intel and older PPC processors.

Step 1: To begin, obtain an installer package from the Python website. To do so, go to https://www.python.org/downloads/ on your Mac; it immediately recognizes your operating system and displays a large button for downloading the newest version of Python installation on your Mac. If it does not, go to the macOS page and select the most recent Python release.

Python »» Downloads »» macOS

Python Releases for macOS

- Latest Python 3 Release - Python 3.10.6
- Latest Python 2 Release - Python 2.7.18

Step 2: Double-click the downloaded file to begin installing Python. The installation process is similar to other macOS apps, with a wizard leading you through the steps. Generally speaking, the default settings are sufficient. To confirm that you want Python installed, your Mac may ask for your password.

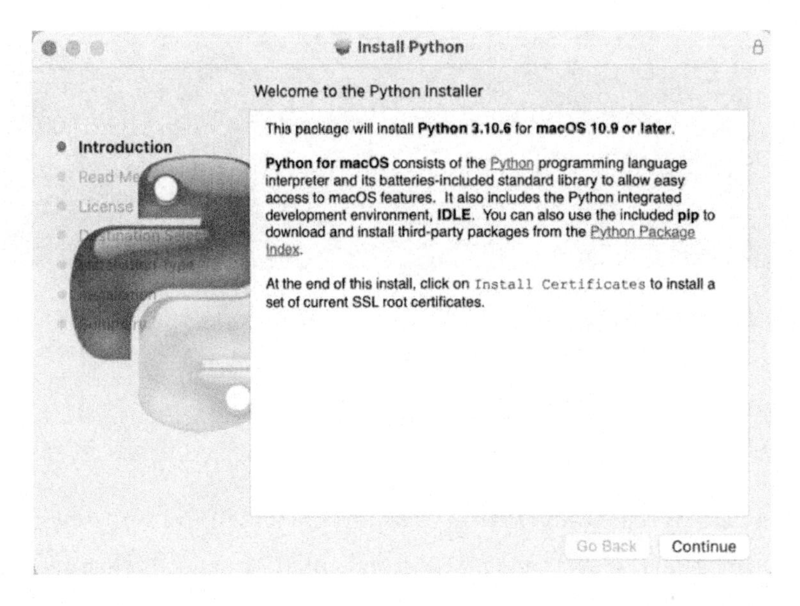

Step 3: After the installation is finished, the Python folder will be opened.

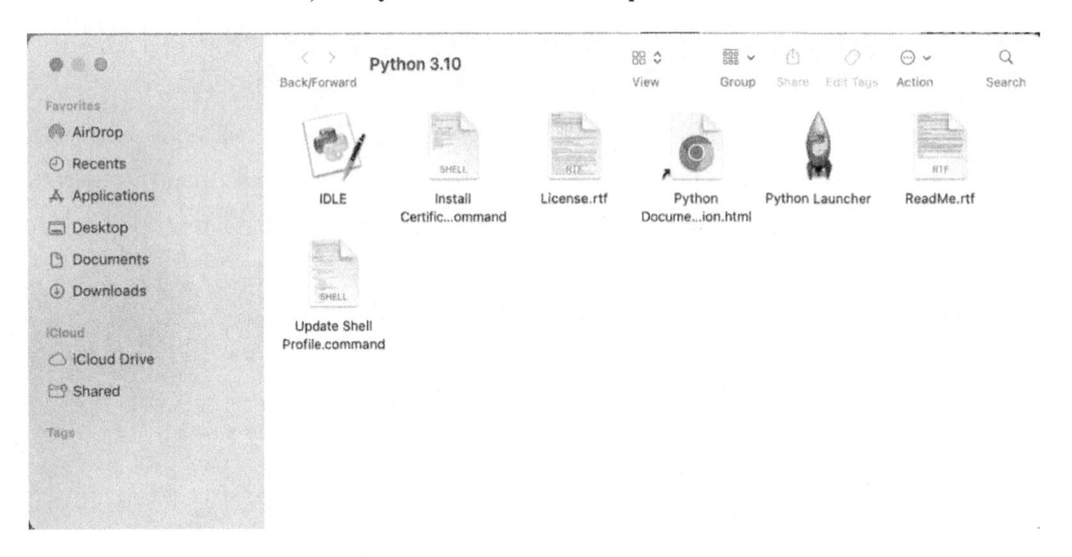

Step 4: To make sure the most recent versions of Python and IDLE (*further discussed in chapter 4*) are properly installed. All it takes is to double-click on Python's integrated development environment (IDLE). IDLE will display the Python shell as follows if everything is set up properly:

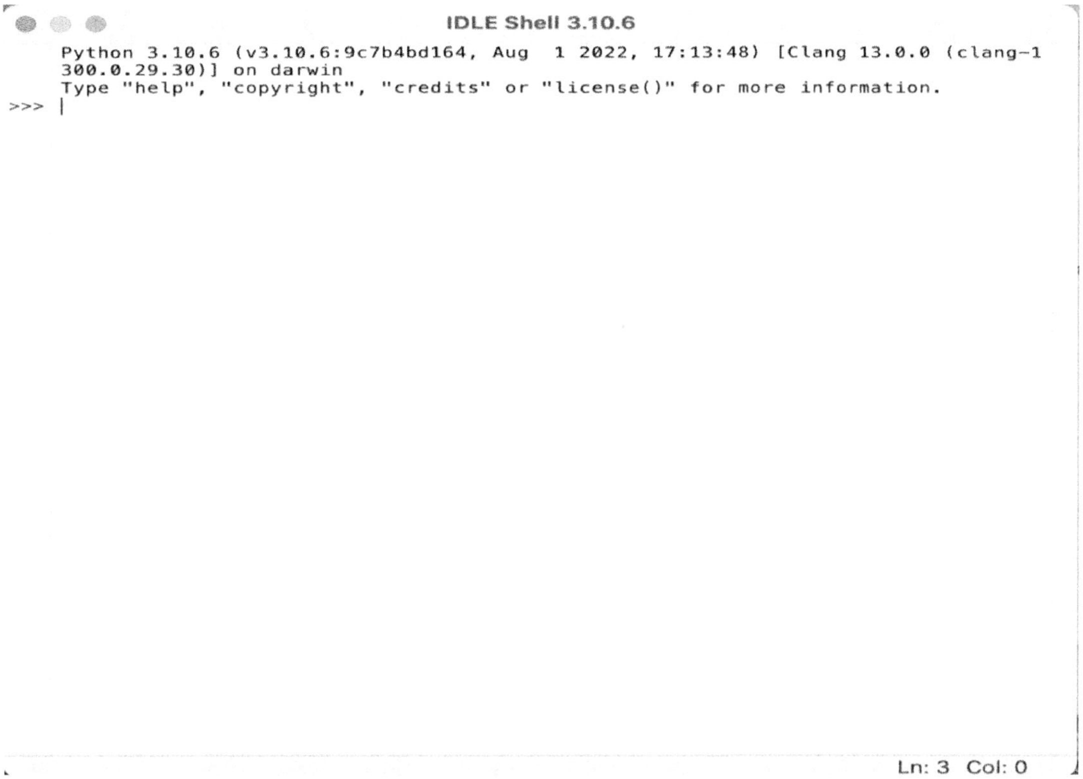

IDLE Shell 3.10.6

```
Python 3.10.6 (v3.10.6:9c7b4bd164, Aug  1 2022, 17:13:48) [Clang 13.0.0 (clang-1
300.0.29.30)] on darwin
Type "help", "copyright", "credits" or "license()" for more information.
>>> |
```

Ln: 3 Col: 0

This confirms that Python has been installed successfully on your macOS machine!

- **Linux**

(*Given below are steps to download Python on Linux*)

Most Python is pre-installed in Linux distributions, while all others offer it as a package. However, some features you might want to utilize are not included in the package for your distro. The most recent Python version can be simply built directly from the origin file.

Step 1: Download the recent Python 3 version from the official Python website. Once the download is finished, you will get ***a.tar.xz*** archive file (sometimes known as a ("*tarball*") containing the Python source code.

Python >>> Downloads >>> Source code

Python Source Releases

- Latest Python 3 Release - Python 3.10.6
- Latest Python 2 Release - Python 2.7.18

Step 2: Once you have downloaded a tarball file, you can extract it by utilizing tools like Linux's tar command or your preferred archive extractor, for instance:

```
$ tar -xf Python-3.?.?.tar.xz
```

Step 3: After extracting the Python tarball, navigate to the configure script and run it in your Linux terminal with:

```
$ cd Python-3.*
./configure
```

The configuration may take some time. Before proceeding, wait till it has been completed successfully.

Step 4: The most recent Python version should now be installed on your Linux machine if no issues have been encountered. Enter one of the following commands on your terminal to confirm it:

```
python --version
```

If the output reads Python 3. x, the Python 3 installation was completed without any problems.

2.3: Difference between Windows, macOS, and Linux

Python programming can be done on either of these operating systems; however, the Mac is significantly quicker than Windows, and Linux is significantly faster than the Mac. As mentioned before, installing Python on any operating system is a rather straightforward process. It is frequently stated that developers created Linux because it was designed to have a good level of integration with many programming languages. On the other hand, Python doesn't change its coding style depending on the situation because it's generally designed for quick tasks that don't require a lot of processing power.

Chapter 3: Python: A Whole New Dimension in Data Types and Variables

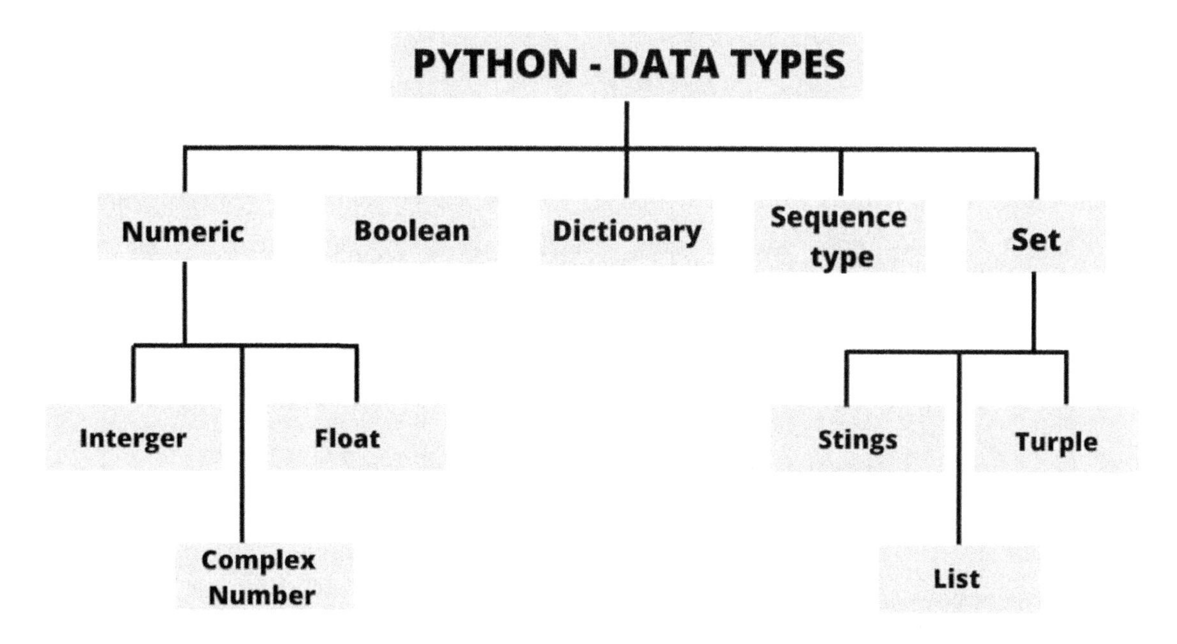

3.1: What is Data Types?

A data type or variable type is a term used in programming that describes the value that variable stores and the kinds of operations that can be carried out without causing an error. In other terms, a data type or variable type defines the kind of value that a variable stores. For instance, a data type known as **int** can be used to represent an integer number, but the data type known as a **string** can be used to describe the text.

3.2: Variables in Python:

In a python program, a variable is similar to a container in which a data value can be stored in the computer's memory. A variable's name may be used to refer to the stored value. A variable declaration has this syntax:

For example, suppose your software requires the user's salary to be stored. To accomplish this, we may call the data **user_salary** and declare the variable **user_salary** as follows:

```
user_salary  = 5000                # stores users' salary as an int.
```

The declaration statement specifies the variable's name first, followed by its value, So the syntax for declaring a variable in Python is:

variable_name = value

This is what makes Python a different programming language from others, as Python is a language with dynamic typing, which implies that the data type of a variable is automatically selected based on the value that is assigned to the variable. This is in contrast to languages such as C# and C++, which are statically typed. As shown in the above example that **user_salary** is **an integer variable**.

Naming a Variable:

In Python, a variable's name can only include letters, numbers, or underscores (_). The first character, cannot be a number. As a consequence, your variables can be called ***userName, user_name***, or ***userName2***, but not ***2userName***. Additionally, such reserved keywords cannot be used as variable names since they already have pre-defined definitions in Python, for instance, **if** and **while.** Finally, variable names in Python are case sensitive, such as ***a*** is not equal to ***A***.

There are different naming schemes for defining a variable; the pythonic way to do it is by using **snake_case** (if the variable consists of two or more words, it will include **'_'**)

3.3: Built-in Data Types in Python:

1. Numerical:

The Python numbers category includes integers and complex numbers, floating points, and other types of numbers. In Python, these values are known as the int, float, and complex classes.

- **int:** Unless there is a physical limitation on the amount of memory, ***an integer*** can be of any length.
- **Float**: A ***floating-point*** number maintains its precision to the 15th decimal place. A decimal point denotes the difference between integers and floating points.

For instance, the number 2 is considered an integer, whereas the number 2.0 is considered a floating-point number.

- **Complex class:** The notation for **complex numbers** is represented as ***a + bj***, where a represents the real component of the number and b represents the imaginary part.

Below are the examples for int, float, and complex classes.

```
x = 6      # is an int
y = 6.4    # is a float
z = 3 + 5j # is a complex number
```

refer to chapter 6 to study more about numbers in Python.

2. String:

The string is how Python and most other programming languages describe the text. The string has Unicode characters. We can use either single quotations or double quotes to represent strings; however, if the strings span many lines, one can use triple quotes such as ''' or """

In the below example, the text Hello World is a single line string; it is written in the double quotation ***"Hello World"*** (alternatively, it could be written in single quotes, such as 'Hello World'). In addition, the text Hello my friend is written in more than one line; hence it is denoted with a triple quotation.

```
txt = "Hello World"
print(txt)
txt = '''Hello my friend'''
print(txt)
```

(To study strings more in dept, refer to Chapter 7)

3. Bool:

Bool, an abbreviation for Boolean and refers to both a conditional and a Binary data type, can only take on one of two potential values: true or false. This data type is commonly used in control flow statements.

```
# this is how to declare a bool in python

my_bool = False
```

4. List:

A list is a numbered or alphabetized set of things. Due to its adaptability and widespread use, it has become a staple of the Python programming language. A list does not necessarily need to include just items of the same kind. The process of declaring a list is simple. Comma-separated lists use brackets **[ ]** to indicate their structure.

```
# list of alphabets

str_list = ['a', 'b', 'c']
```

This list contains three strings: ' a' 'b' and 'c.'

One list might have as many items as one wants, and those objects could be of any variety (integer, float, string, etc.).

```
# list with multiple data types

list = [2, "Hello world", 7.5]
```

This list contains an integer such as ***2***, a string ***"hello world,"*** and a float of ***7.5***

(To study more about lists, you can refer to chapter 11)

5. Tuple:

In Python, a tuple functions similarly to a list. The list items can be modified, whereas those of a tuple cannot be changed after they have been assigned; this is one of the key differences between the two types of data structures.

To build a tuple, enclose each item in parenthesis (), separated by commas. However, the parentheses are optional. A tuple may contain any number of things, which may be of various types (float, int, string, list, etc.).

```
# integers in a tuple
tuple = (3, 6, 9)
print(tuple)
# mixed data types in a tuple
tuple = (4, 'Hello World', 7.6)
print(tuple)
Output:
(3, 6, 9)
(4, 'Hello World', 7.6)
```

It is also possible to construct a tuple without making use of parenthesis. This technique is defined: ***tuple packing***.

```
tuple = 2, 7.8, "cat"

print(tuple)
```

Output:

```
(2, 7.8, 'cat')
```

6. Dictionary

Python's dictionary is a list of items that are not in order. Each item in a dictionary comprises a key and a value. It is easiest to get the value from a dictionary when the key is known. Putting words and phrases inside **curly braces {}** and separating them with commas are all required to create a dictionary. A pair consisting of an item's key and value can be represented in various ways, such as : (key: value).

Keys must be irreversible (string, integer, or tuple with irreversible members) and distinctive.

```
# integer keys in dictionary
dict = {1: 'cat', 2: 'dog'}
# mixed keys in dictionary
dict = {'place': 'New York', 1: [3, 6, 9]}
# using dict()
dict = dict({1:'cat', 2:'dog'})
```

The preceding example demonstrates that the built-in dict() method can also be used to generate a dictionary.

7. Set

A collection of things not arranged in any particular sequence is called a set. We can modify it by including or excluding certain components. Sets can also be utilized to conduct other mathematical set operations such as union, intersection, symmetric difference, and so on.

You can make a set by putting all the elements between **curly braces {}** and separating them with commas, or you can use the **built-in set() function**.

For Example:

```
# Various forms of Python sets

# set of  even integers

set = {2, 4, 6}

print (set)
```

Output

```
{2, 4, 6}
```

(Sets are further discussed in Chapter 10)

Chapter 4: IDLE and Python Shell

4.1: What are IDLE and Python Shell

Python **IDLE** (or IDE) stands for "**Integrated Development and Learning Environment,**" When Python is installed on any system, it comes with various tools to help you code better and be more productive. IDLE comes under those applications or tools that help you write code without downloading anything except Python (If you don't know how to set up Python, refer to chapter two). While many integrated development environments (IDEs) are available, the minimal feature set of Python IDLE makes it ideal for novice programmers.

On the other hand, the **Python Shell** is an interpreter that runs your Python programs and other bits of Python code and commands. The Python Shell permit us to use Python in interactive mode, which means we can enter one command simultaneously. The shell will wait for a command from the operator to execute it and returns the execution result. After this, the shell is waiting for the next command.

4.2: Features of IDLE

- Written entirely in Python with the **Tkinter** graphical user interface toolkit as its primary component.
- Python shell window (collaborative interpreter) with input, output, and error detection colorized according to their respective types.
- Multi-window text editor with several undo, Python syntax colorization, intelligent indenting, call hints, and auto-completion, as well as additional features
- Search within any editor window, replace within editing windows, and search through several files all at the same time
- A debugger that allows for viewing both global and local namespaces, stepping and persistent breakpoints, Dialogue boxes for setup, browsers, and other functions like the settings.
- Cross-platform, which means that it functions similarly on macOS, Windows, and Unix.

4.3: Different IDLE menus:

The **Editor** window and the **Shell** window are the two primary types of windows that IDLE can show. It is possible to open numerous editor windows at the same time. **Windows** and **Linux** each have their own top menus to choose from. There is only one application menu available on macOS. It dynamically adjusts itself depending on which window is currently active. It features an IDLE menu

A subclass of an editor window is known as an **output window**. One example of an output window is the window that appears when you select **Edit > Find** in Files (control + f shortcut key). At the moment, they both have the same top menu, but their default titles and context menus are different.

4.4: Running the Python Shell (without IDLE)

When IDLE is opened, the Python shell automatically starts with it, but there are ways to run the Python shell independently. One way is to use the built-in terminal in your operating system, such as **Command Prompt** (CMD), **PowerShell** on Windows, or **Terminal** on macOS. The process of opening is similar in all of the built-in terminals.

The steps given below will illustrate how to open Python Shell on windows using Command Prompt:

1. On Windows, press the start button on your desktop or press the windows button on your keyboard, or alternatively press the Window button + R, and then search for **CMD:**

   (Using the start button menu)

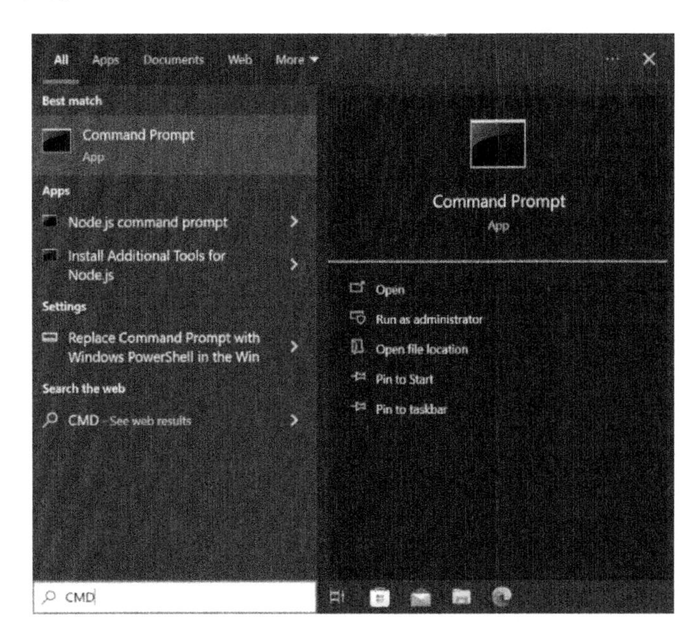

   (Or using the WIN + R)

   (This opens the run)

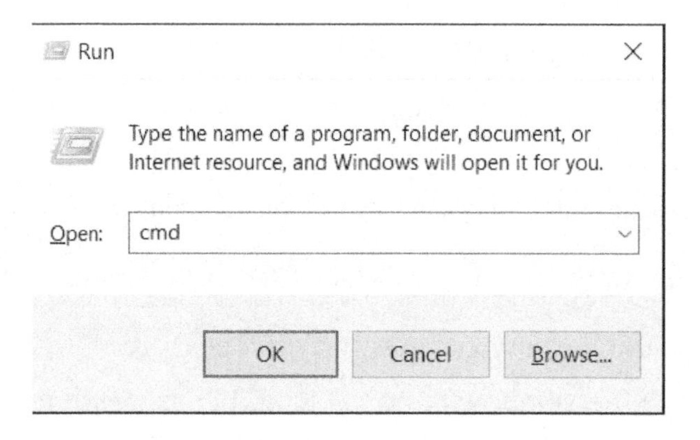

2. Click on open (or press ok if you used windows run program, like the above figure). This will open up a command prompt window.

```
Command Prompt
Microsoft Windows [Version 10.0.19044.1889]
(c) Microsoft Corporation. All rights reserved.

C:\Users\intag>_
```

3. Now, if you have Python installed (if not, refer to Chapter 2), you can type in **Python** in the Command prompt, and A Python Prompt including three greater-than symbols **(>>>)** appears on the screen, as shown in the image below. Now, you can enter a single statement and get the output.

```
Command Prompt - Python

C:\Users\intag>Python
Python 3.10.6 (tags/v3.10.6:9c7b4bd, Aug  1 2022, 21:53:49) [MSC v.1932 64 bit (AMD64)] on win32
Type "help", "copyright", "credits" or "license" for more information.
>>>
```

4. Type the following code:

print ("Hello World!")

```
Command Prompt - Python
Microsoft Windows [Version 10.0.19044.1889]
(c) Microsoft Corporation. All rights reserved.

C:\Users\intag>Python
Python 3.10.6 (tags/v3.10.6:9c7b4bd, Aug  1 2022, 21:53:49) [MSC v.1932 64 bit (AMD64)] on win32
Type "help", "copyright", "credits" or "license" for more information.
>>> print("Hello World!")
Hello World!
>>>
```

The "Hello World!" written after calling the print command is the output!

4.5: Running the IDLE

As discussed above, running the IDLE will automatically open up Python Shell. The user interface is much better than the command prompt, and IDLE is generally more interactive than any terminals (PowerShell, Command Prompt, etc.).

The steps given below will illustrate how to open IDLE on windows:

1. First press the start button or the windows key on your keyboard and search IDLE

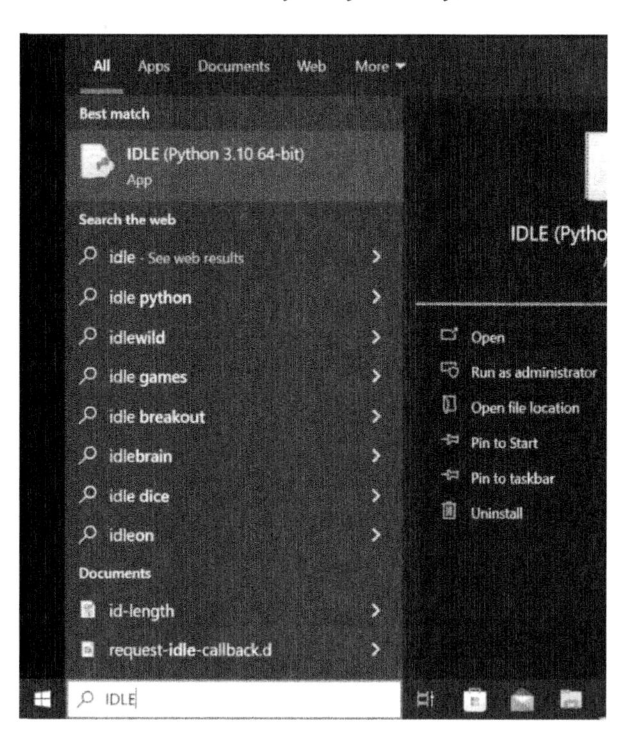

2. Double click or click on open on the right panel. This will open up **IDLE** with Python shell on the window, ready to execute our commands.

```
IDLE Shell 3.10.6                                                          –  □  X
File  Edit  Shell  Debug  Options  Window  Help
    Python 3.10.6 (tags/v3.10.6:9c7b4bd, Aug  1 2022, 21:53:49) [MSC v.1932 64 bit (AMD64)] on win32
    Type "help", "copyright", "credits" or "license()" for more information.
>>> |
```

3. As you can see on the title bar, it says IDLE shell, which means idle is running Python shell, and now we can execute the same code **print ("Hello World!")**

IDLE Shell 3.10.6

File Shell Debug Options Window Help

```
    Python 3.10.6 (tags/v3.10.6:9c7b4bd, Aug  1 2022, 21:53
    Type "help", "copyright", "credits" or "license()" for
>>> print("Hello World!")
    Hello World!
>>> |
```

(The text in blue is output!)

Text file editing and saving are fundamental skills for any programmer. To run Python programs, you need to open a file with the **.py** extension, which contains lines of Python code. Python's integrated development environment (IDLE) makes generating and modifying such files simple.

One huge advantage of Python IDLE is that you'll see several useful features in professional IDEs, such as syntax highlighting, auto-indentation, and code completion which increases our productivity in writing code. Idle is great for learning to code using Python, but it is not recommended when working on our bigger projects using Python. There are better and more professional IDEs in the market. Some of them are: *Visual Studio Code, PyCharm, and* even website-based IDEs such as *Google Collaboratory* are better than IDLE in extensive projects. But these IDEs have a steep learning curve, which is one reason beginners usually prefer to work with IDLE. The other reason is you don't have to download IDLE independently. To follow and practice the code examples in this book, you can use any IDE of your choice.

Chapter 5: Operators in the Python language

5.1: What are Operators?

Every programming language relies on operators as its fundamental building elements. As a result, operators are essential to use the Python language fully. In programming, operators allow us to execute various operations on variables. Python's operators are special symbols used to perform mathematical and logical operations. "operand" refers to the value that is the subject of the operator's action.

For example,

>>> 3+4

7

In this context, the addition operation is denoted by the symbol **+**. *The numbers* **3** *and* **4** *are known as the* ***operands****, and the result is the number* **7**.

The operators in Python are separated into the following categories:

- Arithmetical Operators
- Logical Operators
- Comparison Operators
- Assignment Operators
- Bitwise Operators
- Special Operators (Such as Identity Operators and Membership Operators)

5.2: Arithmetical Operators:

Various mathematical operations, including subtraction, addition, multiplication, and others, can be

conducted with the help of arithmetic operators.

Operative	Implying	Case
+	two operands added (or unary plus)	m+n+3
-	Right operand subtracted from left operand (also known as "unary minus")	m-n-3
/	To achieve this result, simply divide the left by appropriate	m/n

	operand. (the result is always a float)	
*	Multiplication of two operands	m*n
//	Floor division is a type of division that yields whole numbers and shifts the resulting fraction to left direction on the integer line.	m//n
%	Modulus, or the quotient of the left divided by the one on right	m%n (remainder of m/n)
**	Exponent, one exalted to the rank of the other	m**n (m raised to power n)

5.3: Logical Operators:

Operative	Implying	Case
and	Both operands must be true.	m and n
or	True; if one of the two operands evaluates to true	m or n
not	True; if the operand is not true (i.e., complements operand)	not n

The operators **and**, **or**, and **not** are logical operators.

Example *for Logical Operators in the Python programming language:*

```
x = 6
y = 4
# Output: x + y = 10
print('x + y =', x+y)
# Output: x - y = 2
print('x - y =', x-y)
# Output: x * y = 24
print('x * y =', x*y)
# Output: x / y = 1.5
print('x / y =', x/y)
# Output: x // y = 1
print('x // y =', x//y)
# Output: x ** y = 1296
print('x ** y =', x**b)
```

output:

```
x + y = 10
x - y = 2
x * y = 24
x / y = 1.5
x // y = 1
x ** y = 1296
```

```
m = True
n = False
print('m and n is',m and n)
print('m or n is',m or n)
print('not m is',not m)
```

output

```
m and n is False
m or n is True
not m is False
```

The truth table for 'and.'

and will only produce a True result if both of its operands are also True.

A	B	A and B
True	True	True
True	False	False
False	True	False
False	False	False

The truth table for 'or.'

For the case where any of the operands is already True, then the outcome of or will be True. In the following, you will find the truth table for or:

A	B	A and B
True	True	True
True	False	True
False	True	True
False	False	False

The truth table for 'not.'

The 'not' operator is used to do the opposite of what the truth actually is. Below is a truth table containing not operator:

A	Not A
True	False
False	True

Below are a few examples of their usage:

>>> True and False

False

>>> True or False

True

>>> not False

True

5.4: Comparison Operators

In order to compare values, comparison operators are utilized. It will return either True or False depending on whether the condition was met.

Operator	Meaning	Example
>	Greater than: Returns true if the left is bigger than the other operand.	a > b
<	Less than. True if the left is smaller than the right one.	a < b
==	Equal to - True if both operands are equal	a == b
!=	Not equal to - True if operands are not equal	a != b
>=	Greater or equal to: Yields true if the left one is greater or equal to the other operand.	a >= b
<=	Less or equal to: True if left is smaller or equal to right.	a <= b

***Example** for Comparison Operators in the Python programming language:*

```
m = 3
n = 2
# Output: m > n is False
print('m > n is', m>n)
# Output: m < n is True
print('m < n is', m<n)
# Output: m == n is False
print('m == n is',m==n)
# Output: m != n is True
print('m != n is',m!=n)
# Output: m >= n is False
print('m >= n is',m>=n)
# Output: m <= n is True
print('m <= n is',m<=n)
```

output:

```
m> n is False
m < n is True
m == n is False
m != n is True
m >= n is False
```

5.5: Bitwise Operators

Bitwise operators perform their operations on operands as though they were binary digit strings. The term "bit" refers to its operations occurring in discrete increments.

The number 2 in binary represents the number 10, and the number 6 represents the number 110, as just two examples.

The bitwise operators are as follows:

1. **& (bitwise AND):** takes two variables and performs **AND** on each bit of the two variables. **AND** returns 1 only if both variables are **1**.
2. **| (bitwise OR):** takes two variables or operands and performs **OR** on each bit of the two variables. **OR** returns **1** if one of the two bits is **one** or both bits are one.
3. **~ (bitwise NOT):** The number is returned with its complement added.
4. **^ (bitwise XOR):** Uses XOR on each bit of the two numbers provided as operands. The outcome of XOR is 1 if the two bits are distinct.
5. **<< (left shift):** Takes two numbers. Left changes the bits in the first operand or variable and specifies the number of available locations shift in the second variable.

6. **>> (Right shift):** Takes two integers, Modifies the first variable's bits (right), to the number of available locations to move is determined by the second variable.

```
m = 10
n = 4
# Print bitwise AND
print("m & n =", m & n)
# Print bitwise OR
print("m | n =", m | n)
# Print bitwise NOT
print("~m =", ~m)
# print bitwise XOR
print("m ^ n =", m ^ n)
```

output

```
m & n = 0
m | n = 14
~m = -11
 m^ n = 14
# shift operators
x = 10
y = -10
# print bitwise right shift
print("x >> 1 =", x >> 1)
print("y >> 1 =", x >> 1)
x = 5
y = -10
# print bitwise left shift
print("x << 1 =", x << 1)
print("y << 1 =", y << 1)
```

output

```
x >> 1 = 5
y >> 1 = -5
x << 1 = 10
y << = -20
```

5.6: Assignment Operators

In Python, the process of assigning values to variables is accomplished through the use of assignment operators. For example, x=5 is a simple assignment operator that tells the variable x on the left to take on the value 5 on the right. Similarly, Python provides several compound operators, such as x += 5, adding 5 to the variable and then assigning the variable the same value. It is the same as saying that x Equals x + 5.

<table>
<tr><th>Operator</th><th>Example</th><th>Same as</th></tr>
<tr><td>=</td><td>a=5</td><td>a=5</td></tr>
<tr><td>+=</td><td>a += 3</td><td>a = a+3</td></tr>
<tr><td>-=</td><td>a-=3</td><td>a= a-3</td></tr>
<tr><td>*=</td><td>a*=3</td><td>a= a*3</td></tr>
<tr><td>/=</td><td>a/=3</td><td>a= a/3</td></tr>
<tr><td>%=</td><td>a%=3</td><td>a= a%3</td></tr>
<tr><td>//=</td><td>a//=3</td><td>a= a//3</td></tr>
<tr><td>**=</td><td>a**=3</td><td>a= a**3</td></tr>
<tr><td>&=</td><td>a&=3</td><td>a= a&3</td></tr>
<tr><td>|=</td><td>a|=3</td><td>a= a | 3</td></tr>
<tr><td>^=</td><td>a^=3</td><td>a =a^3</td></tr>
<tr><td>>>=</td><td>a>>=3</td><td>a= a>>3</td></tr>
<tr><td><<=</td><td>a<<=3</td><td>A= a<<3</td></tr>
</table>

5.7: Special Operators

The Python programming language has various unique operators, such as identity and membership. They are discussed in detail below, with examples.

- **Identity Operators:**

The terms "**is**" and "**is not**" refer to the identity operators in Python. They are utilized to determine Even if two variables are identical in every other respect, this does not necessarily entail that they are the same.

Operator	Meaning	Example
is	If both operands are the same, then this statement is true.	a is true
is not	If they differ, then this condition is true.	a is not true

***Example** for Identity Operators in Python programming language:*

```
m1 = 6
n1 = 6
m2 = 'Hello World'
n2 = 'Hello World'
m3 = [2,4,6]
n3 = [2,4,6]
# Output: False
print(m1 is not n1)
# Output: True
print(m2 is n2)
# Output: False
print(m3 is n3)
```

output

```
False
True
```

In the above example, m1 and n1 are both integers with the same value, and we can conclude that they are both equal. Equally true with m2 and n2, such as strings. However, we have listed in m3 and n3. In other words, they're comparable but not the same. This is because, despite their equality, the interpreter stores them in different parts of the memory.

- **Membership Operator:**

Python's membership operators are 'in' and 'not in'. They check a sequence for a value or variable (string, list, tuple, set, and dictionary). A dictionary only tests for key, not value

Operator	**Meaning**	**Example**
in	true if sequence contains value/variable	6 in a
not in	This condition will be true if the given value or variable is not present in the given sequence.	6 not in a

***Example** for Membership Operators in Python programming language:*

```
x = ' Hello world '
y = { 1 : 'a' ,2 'b' }

# output: True
print ( 'H' in x )

# output: True
print ( 'hello' not in x )

# output: True
print ( '1' in y )

# output: False
print ( 'a' in y )
```

Output

True

True

True

False

In this situation, x has the letter "H," but it does not contain the word "hello" (as we know, Python is case sensitive). Additionally, in dictionary y, the value for key 1 is the letter 'a. That's why you get a False result when you put 'a' into y.

Chapter 6: Numbers in Python

6.1: What are Numbers?

Numbers are one of the main data types used in any programming language. Math and computer programming aren't as closely tied as some belief, yet numbers are essential to every programming language, including Python. Python has three numeric types representing numbers: integers, floats, and complex numbers. Since they are immutable data types, any attempt to modify the value of a number data type will result in the creation of a new object. We have already discussed these in Chapter 3 as Numerical Data Types; however, in this chapter, we will look at in-depth detail for the numbers in Python.

6.2: Integer Type Numbers

int stands for "integer," which refers to the complete number, including negative numbers but excluding fractions. The length of an integer value has no upper bound regarding Python's support for the data type.

Whole numbers that can be either positive or negative and start with zero are called integers with no fractional components and an unlimited degree of precision. Some examples of integers include 0, 100, and -10.

The following could be the valid integers in Python programming language:

```
>>> 0
0
>>> 100
100
>>> -10
-10
>>> 1234567890
1234567890
>>> a = 4000000000000000000000000000000000000000000000000000
4000000000000000000000000000000000000000000000000000
```

Binary, octal, and hexadecimal numbers are all valid representations of integers in Python.

Binary

In Python, a binary number is a number that starts with 0b, and is made up of 0s and 1s. For example, the binary number 0b11010110 is the same as the integer 214.

```
>>> a =0b11010110>>> a
214
>>> a=0b11010110
>>> a
214
>>> type(a)
<class 'int'>
```

Octal

A representation of an octal number is a number that begins with the prefix 0o or 0O. For instance, the value 20 corresponds to the decimal digit 0O24.

```
>>> a=0o24
>>> a
20
>>> type(a)
<class 'int'>
```

Hexadecimal

Python's hex() function changes an integer into a lowercase hexadecimal string that starts with "0x." We can also give the hex() function an object. If we do this, the object must have a function called __index__() that returns an integer. Hexadecimal numbers are those that begin with the prefix 0x or 0X. The value 60 corresponds to the hexadecimal representation 0x3c.

```
>>> a=0x3c
>>> a
60
>>> type(a)
<class 'int'>
```

6.3: Float Type Numbers

Floating point numbers, abbreviated as a float in Python, are real numbers that can either be positive or negative. They also have a fractional component, which is denoted by the period symbol (.) or the scientific notation E or e, respectively, such as 321.65, 2.341, -1.5, 0.43.

```
>>> f=2.1
>>> f
2.1
>>> type(f)
<class 'float'>
```

We can also differentiate float by using the underscore '_'; for instance, 790_04.873_015 is an actual float.

```
>>> f=790_04.873_015
>>> f
79004.873015
```

The maximum size for a float variable is system dependent. "inf", "Inf", "INFINITY", or "infinity" refers to a float that has been expanded past its maximum size. Most computer systems will treat a float value of 3500 as infinite.

```
>>> f=3e500
>>> f
inf
```

Scientific notation is utilized as a short representation to express floats having several digits. For example: 123.56789 is represented as 1.2356789e2 or 1.23456789E2

```
>>> f=3.4556789e2
>>> f
345.56789
```

We can use the built-in float() function to convert the string, int to float.

```
>>> float('3.5')
3.5
```

6.4: Complex Numbers

The notation for complex numbers in Python is where a represents the real component of the number and b represents the imaginary part.

z = 3 + 5j # is a complex number

You are required to utilize the letter j or J as the imaginary component. If you use any other character, a syntax error will be generated.

```
>>> x=3+2k
SyntaxError: invalid syntax
>>> y=3+j
SyntaxError: invalid syntax
>>> z=7i+2j
SyntaxError: invalid syntax
```

Arithmetic Operators on Integer Values

Different arithmetic operations, as discussed in the table in chapter 4, arithmetic operators could be used on integer values. The addition and subtraction of complex numbers is a straightforward process in which Real and imaginary parts are added/subtracted to get the result. Similarly, the multiplication of two complex numbers is remarkably similar to the multiplication of two binomials.

Chapter 7: String Methods in Python

7.1: What are Methods?

A method is a specific technique of accomplishing or approaching something, especially one that is systematic or established. Each programming language has its definition of methods and functions (more about functions in detail in upcoming chapters). In some cases, both of these words are used interchangeably. For example, in JAVA programming, method and functions mean the same thing.

But in Python programming Methods, those functions are built-in to objects or the data types provided in Python grammar. In other words, a function that "is part of" an object is referred to as its method. In Python, the term "method" is not restricted to being used only with class instances (classes are discussed in detail in chapter 15). Every data type comes with a unique collection of methods. For example, the **list** data type has various helpful methods that can be used to locate values in a list, insert or remove values from a list, and manipulate values in other ways.

In this part of the book, the focus will be on String datatype and its various methods, how to use them, and some real use cases of how built-in methods can be helpful, but before playing around with string methods, let's see how strings work in Python.

7.2: Strings in Python

A **String** is how Python and most other programming languages interpret **text**. In Python, defining a string is rather straightforward. There are two different ways to define a string:

1. **Single Quotes:**

Single quoted strings start and end with a single quotation mark, for example: 'Hello World!'. The issue with single-quoted strings is that what if there is a quote inside the string? For example, consider the following sentence:

'This is Marco's car'

Defining the above sentence as a variable or just printing using the **print()** function will raise an error in Python. Test this example in IDLE:

```
IDLE Shell 3.10.6
    Python 3.10.6 (v3.10.6:9c7b4bd164, Aug  1 2022, 17:13:48) [Clang 13.0.0 (clang-1
    300.0.29.30)] on darwin
    Type "help", "copyright", "credits" or "license()" for more information.
>>> print('this is marco's car')
...
    SyntaxError: unterminated string literal (detected at line 1)
>>> |
```

As you can see, IDLE highlights the last single quote. To solve this issue, we can use double-quoted strings:

2. **Double Quotes:**

Double-quoted strings work the same way as single-quoted strings. The only difference is that strings begin and end with double quotes instead of single quotes. One major advantage of using double quotes instead of single quotes is that the string can contain a single quote character in it. Consider the same example again but instead with double quotes on the outside.

"This is Marco's car"

Again, try printing the above sentence in IDLE using the print() function.

```
IDLE Shell 3.10.6
    Python 3.10.6 (v3.10.6:9c7b4bd164, Aug  1 2022, 17:13:48) [Clang 13.0.0 (clang-1
    300.0.29.30)] on darwin
    Type "help", "copyright", "credits" or "license()" for more information.
>>> print("this is marco's car")
    this is marco's car
```

(The text in blue is output!)

This time the Python and Python shell understand that this is a complete string, and the single quote is a part of it. But let's say you cannot use double quotes, then you'll need to use escape characters.

Escape Character:

Characters that are otherwise impossible to include in a string can be used with the aid of an **escape character**. The character you want to add to the string is followed by a backslash (/), known as an escape character. For example:

'This is Marco's car' will be transformed to ***'This is Marco \'s car'***

Without an escape character, an error will raise, but when the backslash (\) is added, Python will recognize it as a completed string.

```
>>> print('this is marco\'s car')
    this is marco's car
>>> |
```

7.3: String Methods in Python

Now that you are familiar with strings in Python, let's level up and see some useful methods that the string data type provides. As you know by now, Python is a very versatile and flexible language that comes with various functions and commands. It can be quite overwhelming and challenging at times to learn all of them, so this section contains only the most commonly used built-in string methods given below and explained one by one with examples.

*(For this section of the book, the examples were coded using google colabor*atory *instead of IDLE)*

1. **upper() and lower()**

The *upper()* string method converts the whole string to uppercase, for example:

```
name = 'Rick'

print(name.upper())
```

Output:

```
RICK
```

The *lower()* string method converts the whole string to lowercase, for example:

```
name = 'RICK'

print(name.lower())
```

Output:

```
rick
```

Both upper and lower methods return a new value (a new string). We can save this string in another variable like so:

```
name = 'strawberry.'

fruit_name = name.upper()

print(fruit_name)
```

Output:

```
STRAWBERRY
```

2. **len()**

The *len()* is not a string method but a universal function, but it is also very useful with strings. *Len* is shorthand for length. This function returns the length of the string (can also be used with other data types such as lists). Consider the following example

```
fruit_name = 'strawberry.'
print(len(fruit_name))
```

Output:

```
10
```

3. **find**

The *find()* method finds the position (or, in programming, the position is referred to as an index) of a specified letter or string in the given string. Consider the following examples:

```
fruit_name = 'strawberry'
print(fruit_name.find('w'))
```

Output:

```
4
```

Note: The position or index always starts with zero in strings. Strings are a collection of single letters. The letter 'l' is in the 3rd position reading the string from the left side. Now let's consider a complex example:

```
msg = 'Hello! Welcome fellow programmer!'
print(msg.find('fellow'))
```

Output:

```
15
```

In this case, Python only finds the position or index of the first letter of the word you are searching. The 'f' in fellow is at index 15, hence the output. The logic is that behind the find method, Python compares both strings ('fellow' and the **msg** variable).

4. **captalize()**

As its name suggests, the *capitalize()* method gives a string where the first character is capitalized, and the rest are lowercase. Now you can think of a situation where the user enters their name in lowercase, but names always start with an uppercase letter, for example:

```
name = 'richard'
print(name.capitalize())
```

Output:

Richard

5. **casefold()**

The *lower()* string method converts the whole string to lowercase, for example:

```
name = 'MARK'

print(name.casefold())
```

Output:

mark

The difference between *casefold()* and *lower()* is that casefold is stronger, with more accuracy, and more aggressive, which means that it will convert more characters into lower case and will find more correspondences when the strings are confronted when both are converted using the casefold() technique.

6. **count()**

This method gives the number of times a letter (or substring) has appeared in the given string. Consider the example below:

```
quiz = 'how are you darling?'

print(quiz.count('a'))
```

Output:

2

The letter 'a' appeared 2 times in the variable quiz. The count function is case sensitive, meaning if you were to search for the uppercase letter' A', the print function would return zero as output.

7. **replace()**

The *replace()* method is really useful in scenarios where you want to replace something in a string, for example:

```
msg = 'fither'

print(msg.replace("i", "a"))
```

Output:

father

8. **rjust(), ljust(), and center() Methods**

Both the *rjust()* and *ljust()* string methods will return an expanded or spaced version of the string they are called on, meaning that spaces will be added to the string to justify the text. Both of these methods take as their first input an integer representing the desired length of the justified string.

The rjust() refers to right justified, and similarly, ljust() refers to left justified. Try the following commands in Python IDLE or any IDE of your choice:

Code:

```
'right justified.'rjust(25)
```

Output:

```
'right justified'
```

Code:

```
'Left justified'.ljust(25)
```

Output:

```
'Left justified'
```

The ***Center()*** method centers the string by the specified numeric value:

```
'Center alignment'.center(25)
```

Output:

```
Center alignment
```

9. **startswith() and endswith()**

The *startswith()* and *endswith()* methods both return True if the string value that they were called on begins or ends (respectively) with the string that was supplied to the method. If this is not the case, the methods return False. Enter the following into the interactive shell or any integrated development environment.

Code:

```
msg = 'Hello! Welcome fellow programmer!'

print(msg.startswith('Hello'))
```

Output: True

Code:

```
msg = 'Hello! Welcome fellow programmer!'

print(msg.endswith('bye'))
```

Output: False

10. **The is_ methods:**

There are many useful string methods starting with the word "is." The general syntax is "string. is dash()". These are useful in checking certain things. For example, if your string contains digits, you can use **isdigit()** to get a bool (remember bool? true of false only), a commonly used string method starting with the isDash() syntax listed below:

- **isdigit():**

  Returns True if there are digits in the given string.

- **isupper()**

  Returns True if all the letters in the given strings are in uppercase

- **islower()**

  Returns True if all the letters in the given strings are in lowercase.

- **isalpha()**

  Returns True if all the letters in the given strings are alphabets (no digits).

- **isnumeric()**

  Returns True if every character in the given string is numeric.

- **isalnum()**

  Returns True if every character in the given string is alphanumeric.

- **isspace()**

  Returns True if every character in the given string is whitespace. (*In computer programming, whitespace is horizontal or vertical textual space. When rendered, a whitespace character is not visible but occupies page space.*)

- **isdecimal()**

  Returns True if every character in the given string is a decimal number.

- **istitle()**

  Returns True if the given string consists only of words that begin with an uppercase letter followed by only lowercase letters.

- **isprintable()**

  Returns True if the given string is printable

Now let's take a look at the following code example for each of the string methods mentioned above: (*the output is mentioned as a comment in front of each string method being called, and the actual output is given after the code as well*)

Output:

If you run the above code in an IDE of your choice, the output should be something like this:

```
print('1234'.isdigit())    # returns True

print('hello'.isupper())  # returns False

print('BYE'.islower())  # returns False

print('alphabets'.isalpha())        # returns True

print('testing123'.isnumeric())    # returns False

print('Gr8'.isalnum())            # returns True

print('no_spaces_here'.isspace())   # returns False

print('  '.isspace())        # returns True

print('3'.isdecimal())      # returns True

print('not a Title.'.istitle())     # returns False

print('Is This Title Case.'.istitle())    # returns True

print('strings are so fun in Python!'.isprintable())  # returns True
```

```
True
False
False
True
False
True
False
True
True
False
True
True
```

Chapter 8: Program Flow Control in Python

8.1: What is Control Flow?

When a program operates, the sequence in which functions like function calls, instructions, and statements are executed or evaluated is referred to as the program's control flow. You can direct your program's execution using control flow statements, available in many programming languages. In computer programming, the direction of execution is determined by "decision makers." It is possible to make decisions in Python using the if-else elif expression.

Python's control structures can be broken down into three categories:

- **Sequencing**

A sequence of statements is a group of statements whose execution proceeds in a predetermined order. The difficulty with using sequential statements is that the entire source code execution would fail if the logic has broken in only one line.

- **Selection**

In Python, a selection statement can also be referred to as a decision control or branching statement. These are different names for the same construct. With the help of the selection statement, a computer program can evaluate a wide variety of preconditions and, after determining which ones meet the real criteria, can proceed to carry out the necessary steps. The following are examples of decision control statements: if statement, if-else, nested-if, if-elif-else.

- **Repetition**

A group of computer instructions can be repeated by utilizing a statement known as a repetition statement. Two types of loops/repetitive statements are commonly used in Python: **for loop** and **while loop.**

8.2: if statement in Python

The simplest decision-making statement is the **if** statement. It is used to determine if a particular statement or block of statements will be performed or not, i.e., if a specific requirement is satisfied, a block of statements will be executed; otherwise, it will not.

if-statement general syntax:

```
if condition:
   # Statements to execute if
   # condition is true
```

Evaluation of this condition will yield a true or false result. If the statement takes a boolean value, then the block of statements after the statement will be executed if the value is true. The '(' and ')' in a conditional statement are optional.

Python if statement flowchart:

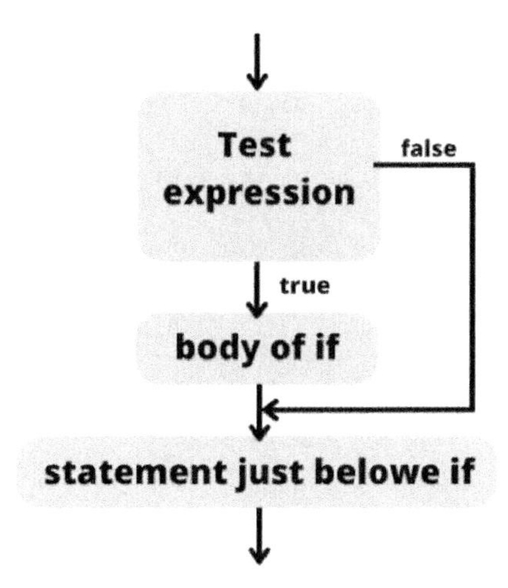

Example to illustrate if statement in Python:

```
x = 7
if (x > 17):
   print("7 is less than 17")
print(" hello Friends ")
```

Output

hello Friends

(Since the if statement's condition is false. As a result, the code is executed after an if statement has evaluated its condition.

8.3: if-else statement in Python:

The if statement alone tells us that if a condition is true, a block of statements will be executed; if the condition is false, the block of statements will not execute. But if the condition is false, then the else statement will follow. When the condition is false, we may use the else statement in conjunction with the if statement to execute a code block.

if-else statement general syntax:

```
if (condition):
   # Executes this block if
   # condition is true
else:
   # Executes this block if
   # condition is false
```

Python if-else statement flowchart:

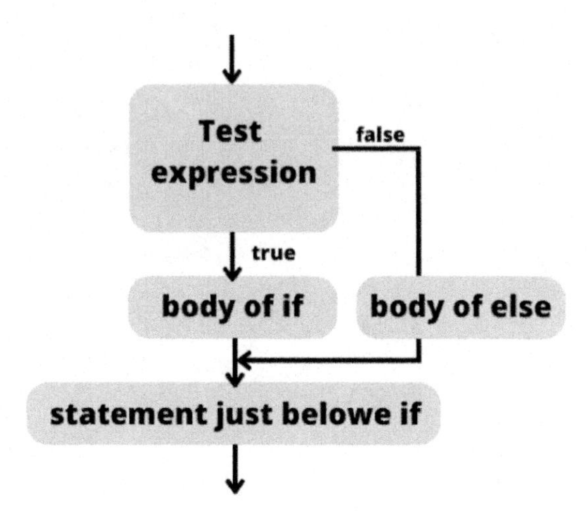

Example to illustrate if-else statement in Python:

```
# Program checks if the number is positive or negative
# And displays an appropriate message

num = 3

# Try these two variations as well.
# num = -5
# num = 0

if num >= 0:
    print("Positive or Zero")
else:
    print("Negative number")
```

Output:

```
Positive or Zero
```

In the above example, we can see that when the number is equal to 3, the expression reads it as ***true*** *and results in the execution of the if-body and* ***else*** *is omitted. However, when the number is equal to -5, the expression is read as* ***false****,* here, the **else statement** is executed and **if** is skipped. Furthermore, when the number is equal to 0, the expression is **true** here **if** it is executed and **else** is executed.

8.4: if-else-elif statement in Python:

In an if-else-elif statement, a user can make a number of choices. The **if statement** runs in reverse order. When an if statement's condition evaluates to true, the sentence it refers to is carried out; the rest of the ladder is skipped over. The last **else statement** will be carried out if none of the preceding ones are satisfied.

if-else-elif general syntax:

```
if  expression:
   if-body
elif expression:
   elif-body
else:
   else-body
```

Python if-else-elif statement flowchart:

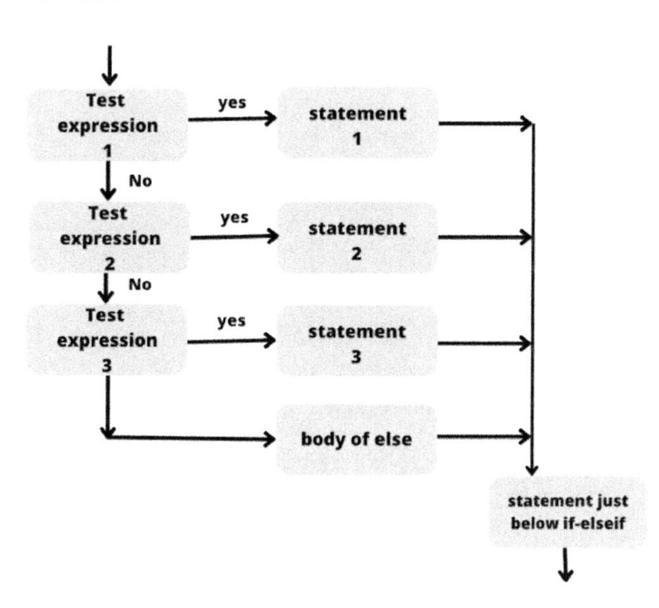

Example to illustrate if-else-elif statement in Python:

```
a= 20
if (a == 10):
   print("a is 10")
elif (a == 15):
   print("a is 15")
elif (a == 20):
   print("a is 20")
else:
   print("a is not present")
```

Output:

a is 20

8.5: Nested if statement in Python

There can be an if-elif-else statement inside of another if-elif-else statement. In computer science, this technique is known as **nesting**. Such sentences can be layered as many levels deep as desired. To determine the depth of nesting, **indentation** must be used. Avoid them unless required because of the potential for confusion.

if-else-elif statement general syntax:

```
if (condition a):
    # Executes when condition a is true
    if (condition b):
        # Executes when condition b is true
    # if block ends here
# if block ends here
```

Python-if.else statement flowchart:

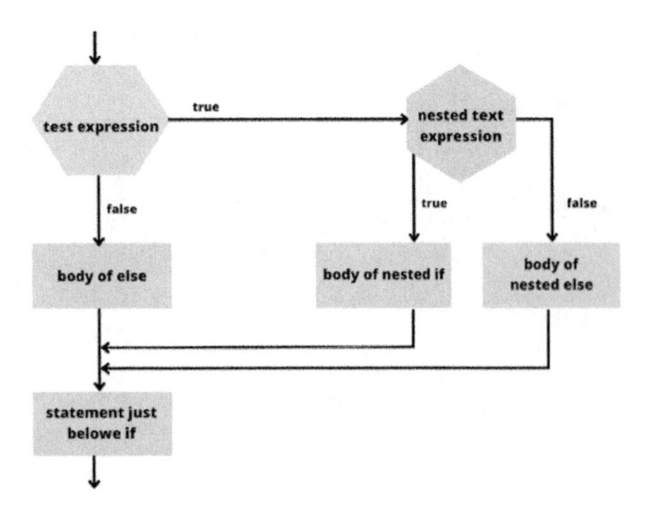

Example to illustrate Python nested if:

```
x= float(input("Enter an integer: "))
if x >= 0:
   if x == 0:
      print("Zero")
   else:
      print("Positive number")
else:
   print("Negative number")
```

First output

Enter a number: 0

Zero

Second output

Enter a number: 6

Positive number

Third output

Enter a number: -2

Negative number

8.6: Repetition Statement

- for loop

It is possible to iterate over a sequence using a for loop, regardless of whether the sequence is a list, tuple, dictionary, or set. We can run a group of statements just once for each item contained in a list, tuple, or dictionary. Here is the flow chart for the loop in the python programming language.

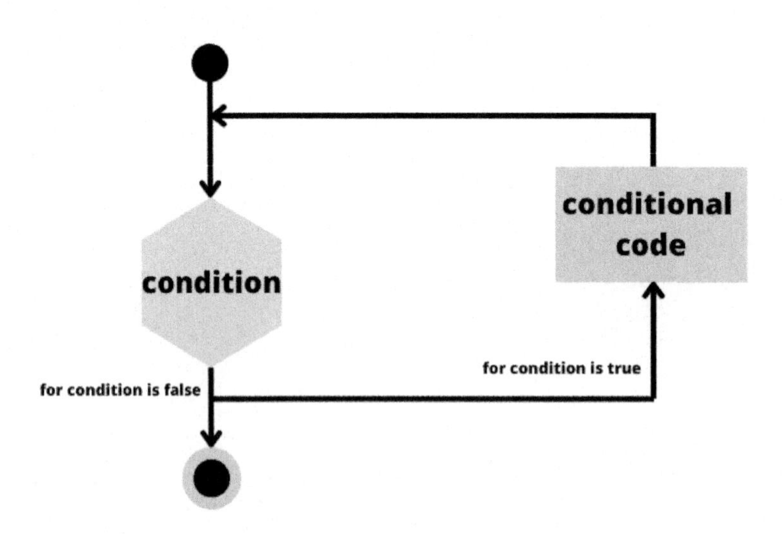

- while loop

Python's while loops are used to continually execute a block of statements until a certain condition is met. This can take a long time. After that, the expression is examined again; if it has not changed, the body is carried out a second time. This process will continue until the expression is shown to be incorrect. Below is the flow chart for the while loop in python programming.

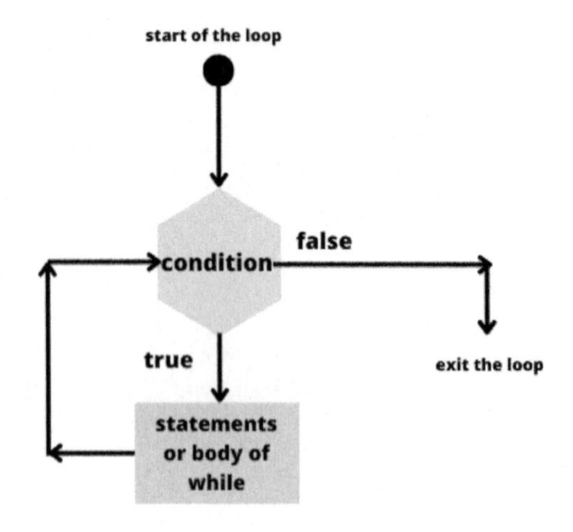

Chapter 9: Functions in Python

9.1: What are Functions?

A function is a block of code that is only executed when it is called, and calling a function is also known as invoking the function.

The use of functions allows our program to be broken into more manageable and modular chunks. As the size of our program continues to expand, the addition of functions enables us to organize better and control it. In addition, it helps keep the code reusable and eliminates unnecessary repetition. Until this part of the book, you should be familiar with the basic ***print()*** function and the string methods we discovered in Chapter 7. Now we will look at more helper functions provided by the Python programming language, such as the famous and commonly used **input()** function and other built-in functions.

Before diving deep into the world of functions, let's look at the structure and terminologies surrounding a function.

What is an Argument:

The argument is the value sent to the function when it is called. In this case, the string "Hello World!" is being passed to the print function as an argument.

As you might have figured out, there are two major types of functions in Python:

1. *Built-in functions*
2. *User-defined functions*

9.2: Printing and Getting User Input

Python, as we know, is a bundle of various tools and pre-defined logic to help programmers to focus more on building stuff. For this purpose, Python already has a cluster of built-in functions. Commonly used built-in functions are given below:

1. **The print() function:**

    In previous chapters, we have seen different print function uses. The main purpose of print is to get an output of given instruction to the Python shell. As an analogy, imagine using a calculator, and the program asks for two numbers. After you've entered the numbers, the calculator program will return a sum or result of any other mathematical operation. You see the result on the screen using the **print()** function.

    Now let's create a simple program for adding two numbers:

```
x = 9
```

```
y = 8
s = x + y
print(s)
```

Output:

```
17
```

Now let's extend the program by allowing the user to enter the numbers using the **Input()** function.

2. **The input() function:**

As the name suggests, the input function gets user input. To understand the usage better, take a look at the code below, which is an extended version of the previous example:

```
x = input("Enter first number: ")
y = input("Enter second number: ")
s = x + y
print("The sum is: ", s)
```

Output:

The output of the above code snippet will be first like this:

```
Enter the first number:
```

The code will first ask for the first number. After the user enters a number, it will save that value in the associated variable. In this case, the variable x. After that, the terminal or shell will ask for the input of the second variable (y). when the user enters the second number, the code will move to the next line and adds both x and y variables entered by the user, then print the result using the print function.

Using the **input** function like this will result in **incorrect answers**. Now let's completely run the code and see the **issue**.

```
x = input("Enter first number: ")
y = input("Enter second number: ")
s = x + y
print(s)
```

Output:

Let's assume that the user entered the first number as 5 and the second number as 3:

```
Enter first number: 9
```

Enter second number: 8

The sum is: 98

As you can see, the sum is incorrect, and this is because the **input** function in Python, by default, returns **string** data type. As a result of adding the variables, we are getting concatenated or the addition of two strings. This issue introduces the concept of **typecasting** data types.

9.3: Typecasting in Python

Typecasting is the process or ability to change or convert the data type of a value to another data type.

In Python, this is easily achievable using built-in typecasting functions. Let's continue our previous example of using the input function. As you know, the **input** function in Python returns a string even if the user enters a number. We can use built-in (or pre-defined) **typecasting** functions provided by Python:

```
x = input("Enter first number: ")

y = input("Enter second number: ")

s = int(x) + int(y)

print("The sum is: ", s)
```

In the above example, we take user input before the addition operation happens, the variables are converted, or in programming, the terminology is typecasted into integer type from string data type. The result of the above code is if the user enters **x = 9** and **y = 8**.

Output:

Enter first number: 9

Enter second number: 8

The sum is: 17

Which is the correct result. Similarly, we can use other pre-defined typecasting functions to convert to other data types. For converting to string, we can use the **str()** function and **float()** to convert to numbers that include a floating or decimal point. Take a look at the following code example, which has comments showcasing the result of calling the respective functions:

```
x = 1       # int
y = 6.9     # float
z = "3"     # string
# Typecasting y to an int:
  int(y)     # this is not a permanent change as we are not saving the value in a variable
x = float(x)
# Permanently change y to an int:
y = int(y)
# Changing z to int
z = int(z)
# y to string;
y = str(y)
print(x)        # outputs 1.0
print(y)        # outputs 6
print(z + 6)   # output 9
# example for type casting (from int to str):
print("X is equal to " + x)         # This will raise an error and will need to convert x to a string to
add two strings
print("X is equal to " + str(x))
# Outputs: X is equal to 1.0
```

Now Typecasting is out of the way. Let's look at other popular built-in functions apart from **print** and **input.**

9.4: Popular built-in functions.

This section covers some of the useful and probably the common built-in functions developers use in their projects:

- **abs()**

The abs() function returns the absolute value of the given number (the size of a real number without regard to its sign is known as absolute values in mathematics)

```
num = -38

absolute_number = abs(num)

print(absolute_number)
```

Output:

38

- **min()**

The min() function finds and returns the minimum number between two givens numbers as arguments.

print(min(1,5))

Output: 1 as 1 is the minimum out of the given numbers

- **max()**

The min() function finds and returns the maximum or largest number between two given numbers as arguments.

print(max(1, 5))

Output: 5 as 1 is the minimum out of the given numbers.

- **sum()**

When working with lists or any object which can be looped or iterated with the help of a loop (*Programming terminology*: a **loop** is an iterative series of instructions that runs over and over again until a predetermined condition is met), check the following example (In this example we are working with lists which is a data type described in Chapter 3 and are explored in more detail in chapter 11)

```
numbers_list = [1,2,3,4,5]
# start parameter is not provided
Sum = sum(numbers_list)
print(Sum)
# start = 5
Sum = sum(numbers_list, 5) # the 5 here is the starting number added to all  of the numbers in the list
that is : 5 + 1 + 2 + 3 +  4 + 5 = 20
print(Sum)
```

Output:

15

20

- **eval()**

This is a handy function to solve string expressions. The eval() function takes an expression as its argument, analyzes it, and executes that parsed expression as Python code within the application.

```
num = 3

# eval performs the multiplication passed as an argument

square_num = eval('num * num')

print(square_num)
```

Output:

9

Can you think about more use cases of the **eval()** function?

Python is a vast programming language with a lot of helpful pre-defined functions. As this book is targeted toward beginner programmers, we are not going to cover all of the built-in functions, but if you're still interested to learn more about Python, the best resource is to learn more from the official documentation of Python and for built-in functions check the following link: https://docs.Python.org/3/library/functions.html

9.5: User-defined functions

User-defined functions are the custom functions created or defined by the programmer. Custom functions are useful in many scenarios, such as code repetition, and these also help in better organization of the whole code. Let's take a look at the structure of defining a custom function and the keywords involved.

This figure shows a basic structure of defining a custom function. The first keyword **def** is short for define, which is used to define the function name and start. The word **function** here can be anything (naming clear and concise functions and variable helps in the long run!). Take notice of the indention before the word **pass** (in Python, the pass doesn't do anything and mostly is used as a placeholder, when the function in the above figure is called, there is no output).

Now take a look at the following examples.

```
def multi_hello():
    print("Hello there")
    print("Hello World!")
    print("Hello Hi")
multi_hello()
multi_hello()
```

Output:

```
Hello there
Hello World!
Hello Hi
Hello there
Hello World!
Hello Hi
```

The advantage here is clear, you can achieve the same result by using the **print(),** but the code will look spammy and unorganized. So, by defining a function, we can reduce the number of lines and code repetition and help in readability. The code below is given for an addition function that adds two numbers:

```
def add():
 return 8 + 4
print(add())
```

Output:

12

The **return** is another commonly used keyword in Python and programming. In general, this keyword is used to return any values, but it does not print or show those values in the output panel/console

The above **add** function will only work for the hardcoded values given in the code (in this case, 8 and 4), but what if you want to add other numbers as well? This question leads to one of the popular concepts: **parameters** in functions:

What are the Parameters?

A parameter is a variable registered inside the parentheses in the function definition. The terms parameter and argument can be used for the same thing: values or information passed into a function. In Python, we call it a parameter while defining, and when calling the function, we call it an argument. Take a look at the structure of the function with parameters:

In Python 3.7+, there is no limit to the number of parameters in a function, but it is not recommended to have many parameters; keeping track of all of them could be hectic. Let's now add parameters to the **add function**

```
def sum(first_num, second_num):
   return first_num + second_num
print(sum(1, 4))
print(sum(7, 4))
print(sum(4, 8))
```

Output:

5

11

12

Inside custom functions, you can also define variables. These variables are called **local variables,** and the variables outside the function body are called **global variables.**

Chapter 10: Sets in Python

10.1: What is a Set?

*A collection of things not arranged in any particular sequence is called a **set**.*

We can modify it by including or excluding certain components. Sets can also be utilized to conduct other mathematical operations such as **union** and **intersection**.

10.2: Defining a Set in Python

You can make a set by putting all the elements between curly braces **{}** and separating them with commas, or you can use the built-in **set()** function.

Now let's take a look at the code:

```
my_set = {2, 4, 6}
print(my_set)
```

Output:

{2, 4, 6}

Sets can also contain mixed data types, excluding lists, sets, and dictionaries:

```
mx_set = {8.0, "even", (2, 4, 6)}
print(mx_set)
```

This will again print all of the contents of mx_set. Another thing to take notice of is that sets cannot have duplicated values:

```
set = {1, 2, 3, 1}
print(set)
```

Output : {1, 2, 3}

If there is duplicated value, it will be ignored.

Creating a set with no elements in it can sometimes be difficult. Python code enclosed in empty curly braces will produce an empty dictionary. We use the set() function with no arguments to create a set that does not contain any elements.

```
x = {}
#  data type of a
print(type(x))
# initialize a set using method set()
y = set()
# checking data type of a
print(type(y))
```

Output:

```
<class 'dict'>

<class 'set'>
```

10.3: Changing a set in Python

As we already know, sets in Python are mutable (which means we can change the data inside a set). Sets are also unordered, so there is no direct access to each element by using the index value or position of the element (more about indexes in the next chapter).

Python again provides us with useful methods with sets for updating and removing. First, let's look at **adding** new elements to a set.

Adding new elements to a set:

There are two methods we can use to add new elements to a set:

1. **add()**

The add() method is used to add a single new element to a set. Duplicated values are ignored

```
even_set = {4, 6, 8, 2}
even_set.add(0)
print(even_set)
```

Output:

{0, 2, 4, 6, 8}

1. **update()**

Update function is used to add multiple elements to a set. As its argument, the update() method can accept tuples, lists, strings, or any other kind of set. And again, duplicated values are ignored.

```
even_set = {4, 6, 8, 2}
even_set.update({0, 12, 10})
print(even_set)
```

Output:

{0, 2, 4, 6, 8, 10, 12}

Removing elements from a set:

Python provides four methods for removing elements from a set:

1. **discard()** and **remove()**

The discard() and remove() methods both allow for the removal of a single item from a set ().

The sole distinction is that the discard() method does not alter the set if the element is not contained within it. However, in this case, the remove() method will throw an error (if the element is not present in the set).

```
# discard vs remove
# define set 'a'
x = {2, 6, 3, 5, 8}
print("original set", x)
# discard an element
x.discard(3)
print("3 is discarded", x)
# remove an element
x.remove(5)
print("5 is removed", x)
# discard an element which is not present in x
x.discard(1)
print("1 is discarded (even though there is no 1 in set x this function is still being executed)", x)
# remove an element which is not present in x
# you will get an error.
x.remove(1)
```

Output:

```
original set {2, 3, 5, 6, 8}
3 is discarded {2, 5, 6, 8}
5 is removed {2, 6, 8}
1 is discarded (even though there is no 1 in set x this function is still being executed) {2, 6, 8}
Traceback (most recent call last):
 line 24, in <module>
  x.remove(1)
KeyError: 1
```

2. **pop()**

The pop() method allows us to remove and return an item.

It is impossible to predict which item will be popped from a set because sets are not ordered. It is entirely random.

```
x = {2, 6, 3, 5, 8}
print("original set", x)
print(x.pop())
print(x)
```

Output:

```
original set {2, 3, 5, 6, 8}
2
{3, 5, 6, 8}
```

3. **clear()**

The clear method is used to remove or delete all of the elements of the set.

```
x = {2, 6, 3, 5, 8}
print("original set", x)
x.clear()
print(x)
```

Output:

```
original set {2, 3, 5, 6, 8}
set()
```

10.4: Operations on Sets

Sets can be handy for mathematical operations such as intersection, union, symmetric difference, and set difference. Python provides methods to apply these operations, and we also have the choice of using operators.

Union:

Union operation means combining two sets. This can be achieved by using the single OR (|) operation or the **union()** method:

```
even_set = {2, 4, 6}
odd_set = {1, 3, 5}
# using | operator
print(even_set | odd_set)
# using union method
print(even_set.union(odd_set))
```

Output

```
{1, 2, 3, 4, 5, 6}
{1, 2, 3, 4, 5, 6}
```

Intersection:

Intersection means selecting the common elements from both sets. We use the and (&) operator to perform an intersection. The **intersection()** method can accomplish the same thing.

```
a_set = {2, 4, 6}
b_set = {1, 3, 2}
# using and operator
print(a_set & b_set)
# using union method
print(a_set.intersection(b_set))
```

Output

```
{2}
{2}
```

2 is returned as it is in both sets.

Set Difference

Returns the elements only in the first but not in the second set. The minus (-) operator and the difference() method are used to achieve this:

```
a_set = {2, 4, 6}
b_set = {1, 3, 2}
# using and operator
print(a_set - b_set)
# using union method
print(a_set.difference(b_set))
```

Output:

{4, 6}

{4, 6}

Symmetric Difference

Symmetric difference returns a set that doesn't include the common elements of both sets.

```
a_set = {2, 4, 6}
b_set = {1, 3, 2}
# using and operator
print(a_set ^ b_set)
# using union method
print(a_set.symmetric_difference(b_set))
```

Output:

```
{1, 3, 4, 6}
{1, 3, 4, 6}
```

Chapter 11: Lists in Python

11.1: What is a List?

A list is a numbered or alphabetized set of things. Due to its adaptability and widespread use, it has become a staple of Python.

11.2: Defining a List

The process of declaring a list is simple. Comma-separated lists use brackets [ ] to indicate their structure.

In code:

```
# list of alphabets
str_list = ['a', 'b', 'c']
# mixed list
mx_list = [2, "Hello world", 7.5]
```

As you can see, a list does not necessarily need to include the same data type elements.

The major difference between sets and Lists is that sets cannot have multiple occurrences of the same element, and lists have indexing, allowing us to access and modify elements.

11.3: Accessing elements in a List

Indexing in a list refers to selecting or accessing single elements in a list or accessing multiple elements using loops as lists are iterable.

When we want to access a specific item in a list, we can use the index operator **[ ]**. When working with Python, indices always begin at 0. Therefore, the index for a list with ten items will range from zero to nine (ten in total). You can also define a list within another list (nested lists). Accessing the nested list requires nested indexing.

An **IndexError** will be generated if you attempt to access indexes other than these. It is required that the index be an **integer**. We cannot utilize float or any other data types because doing so will generate a **TypeError**.

```
vowels = ['a', 'e', 'i', 'o', 'u']
# first element
print(vowels[0]) # a
# fourth element
print(vowels[3]) # o
#example of a list within a list
the_list = ["Testing", [1, 2, 3]]
print(the_list[0][0])
print(the_list[1][1])
# TypeError! Only integers can be used for indexing
print(vowels[4.0])
```

Output:

```
a

o

T

2

Traceback (most recent call last):

  line 18, in <module>

    print(vowels[4.0])

TypeError: list indices must be integers or slices, not float
```

Python also allows negative indexes, unlike many other programming languages. An item with an index of -1 is the very last one in the list; an item with an index of -2 is the second to last, and so on.

11.4: Changing elements of a list

Similar to sets, lists are also mutable, meaning you can add, remove and update the elements of a list. The easiest way to do this is by using the assignment operator =. Take a look at the example below:

```
# this list contains a letter that is not a vowel. Lets fix this

vowels = ['a', 'e', 'i', 'o', 'l']

# we know that the letter 'l' is at index 4

vowels[4] = 'u'
```

print(vowels)

Output: ['a', 'e', 'i', 'o', 'u']

Lists like sets come with various methods to modify their content methods. The append() method is used for adding a single element, and extend() is used for adding multiple elements at once. **insert()** is another method that is used for inserting. The **Python del statement** is used to delete a single and multiple elements, or we can completely delete the list using the del statement.

The methods pop() and remove() are available for removing a single element from a list. This time, **pop()** works a little differently than how it works in a set. The difference is if no index is given, the **pop()** method discards the last item and returns it. To delete all the elements of a list, the **clear()** method is used. The code given below showcases all of these methods.

Code: for adding new elements to a list

```
even = [2, 4, 6]
even.append(8)    # adding a single value at a new
last index
print(even)
even.extend([12, 14]) # adding multiple values
print(even)
even.insert(4, 10)  # inserting 10 at 4th index
print(even)
```

Output:

```
[2, 4, 6, 8]
[2, 4, 6, 8, 12, 14]
[2, 4, 6, 8, 10, 12, 14]
```

Code: for deleting elements from a list

```
even = [2, 4, 6, 8, 10, 12, 14]
del even[3] # delete element at index 3
print(even)
even.pop()  # pops the last element
print(even)
even.remove(10) # removes 10 from the list
print(even)
```

Output:

```
[2, 4, 6, 10, 12, 14]
[2, 4, 6, 10, 12]
[2, 4, 6, 12]
```

11.5: Usage of Lists

Lists are really useful in **Data structures** (this topic is out of scope for this book as this is targeted toward beginners). Other uses of the list data type are to make a collection of similar things in a program. Suppose your program needs a lot of numbers of the same or mixed data type, and you also need to know their position so you can access those numbers directly. Then the easiest way to organize would be by using lists.

Lists are the foundation for data structures. You can implement stacks, queues, and linked lists. Implementing a stack is very easy using a Python list as we already have the methods **pop()** and **append()**

Chapter 12: Modules in Python

12.1: What are Modules?

A code library or a file that includes a set of functions that you want to include in your application are both examples of modules. If we want to keep things straightforward, we may consider a module the same as a code library. Modules are simple files with the ". py" suffix that contains Python code and may be imported into another Python program. Using modules, we can group related functions, classes, or code blocks in the same file. Large Python code blocks should be divided into modules containing 300–400 lines of code, as this is the best approach for creating larger programs. A file with Python code, such as addition.py, is called a module, and that module's name would be an **addition**.

To understand modules in Python, you can write the following code and name it **addition.py.**

```
def add(x, y):
    sum = x + y
    return sum
```

*In this case, an example module contains the **add() function**. The input of two numbers is used to calculate and then return the total of those numbers by the function.*

Components in a Module:

- Classes,
- Variables,
- Functions are defined and implemented so that they may be called and utilized from within another application.

12.2: Importing Modules:

It is possible to use the definitions from one Python module in another or even in the interpreter itself, owing to the language's modular structure. To accomplish this, we make use of the **import keyword**. To import the module example we have already defined, type the following into the python prompt.

```
>>> import addition
```

*The names of the functions created in the example are not automatically added to the current symbol table. The module's name is the only thing that gets imported. If we know the module's name containing the desired function, we may use the **dot (.) operator** to call that function. Here's an illustration:*

```
>>> addition.add(2,1)
3
```

*There is a tonne of standard modules available for Python. You can view the Python standard modules and the contexts in which they are used. These files can be found in the Lib directory of the place where Python was installed on your computer. Python's **NumPy** module is one of its most popular and commonly utilized modules.*

Standard modules are imported like user-defined modules. Importing modules is straightforward. Some are listed below.

Import statement in Python:

Once a module has been imported with the import statement, its definitions can be accessed with the dot operator. Here's a case in point:

```
import math as m

print("The value of pi is", m.pi)
```

output

The value of pi is 3.141592653589793

*According to the above illustration, the **math module** is now known as **m**. In certain situations, this will allow us to spend less time typing. Please note that we do not cover anything under the heading "math." Since math.pi is not valid, the proper implementation is m.pi.*

From-Import to Python:

It is also possible to import only a subset of a module's names without actually importing the entire module. Here's a case in point.

```
# only importing pi from the math module

from math import pi

print("The value of pi is", pi)
```

The **dot(.)operator** is not used under these conditions. This also allows us to import several attributes at once:

```
>>> importing pi, e from math
>>> pi
3.141592653589793
>>> e
2.718281828459045
```

Importing all Names

The following construct imports all module names (definitions):

```
# Importing all names from the m standard module

from math import *

print("The value of pi is," pi)
```

All of the math module's definitions have been imported into this section. This covers all names visible within our scope, except those whose first characters are underscores (private definitions).

(Programming best practices recommend avoiding the habit of prefixing import statements with an asterisk (*). This can result in many definitions being assigned to a single identifier. In addition, it makes our code more difficult to read.)

12.3: Module Search Path in Python:

Python checks numerous areas when importing a module. The interpreter starts with **built-in** modules. Python checks **sys.path** if no built-in module is found. The search is in this order.

- Current directory.
- Pythonpath (an environment variable with a list of directories).
- Default installation directory.

```
• >>> import sys
• >>> sys.path
• ['',
• 'C:\\Python33\\Lib\\idlelib',
• 'C:\\Windows\\system32\\python33.zip',
• 'C:\\Python33\\DLLs',
• 'C:\\Python33\\lib',
• 'C:\\Python33',
• 'C:\\Python33\\lib\\site-packages']
```

This list is open for additions and alterations so we can include our way.

12.4: Module reloading:

An individual session of the Python interpreter only ever imports a module once. Because of this, we can accomplish more in less time. Here's a case study to illustrate the principle in action. Let's pretend there is some code in a module we'll call module_one.

print("executing this code")

output

>>> import module_one

executing this code

>>> import module_one

```
>>> import module_one
```

We can see that only one time was our code run. This means that our module was only brought in once. During the program, if our module changed, we would have to reload it. Restarting the interpreter is one way to do this. But this doesn't do much to help. This can be more quickly accomplished with Python. We can use the reload() function in the imp module to reload a module. Here are some ways to do it:

```
>>> import imp

>>> import module_one

executing this code

>>> import module_one

>>> imp.reload(module_one)

executing the code

<module 'module_one' from '.\\module_one.py'>
```

The Built-in dir () Function:

The **directory()** function allows us to discover module-specific names using a module's import list. For instance, we defined an add() function in the initial module example.

Chapter 13: File Handling in Python

13.1: What is File Handling?

File handling refers to managing files which includes creating, writing, and reading data in a file.

In other words, programming is not complete without file handling. Python's built-in methods make common file-related tasks much more manageable, such as creating, opening, and closing files. In addition to reading, writing, and appending data while files are open, Python permits various file handling operations.

13.2: File Handling in Python.

As mentioned in the intro, Python provides built-in methods to make common tasks easier. The steps of a file operation are as follows:

1. Open a file.
2. Write or read.
3. Save and close the file.

Opening a file using Python:

Python has a built-in function called **open()** to open a file. A file object (also known as a handle) is returned when executed.

```
file1 = open("doc.txt")    # opening a file in the same directory
file2 = open("C:/PythonSripts/another.txt") # specifying full path
```

The open function also comes with several **modes**. When a mode is specified, the file is opened in the correct state for that operation, for instance, for read operation the **r** and for writing **w.** All of the modes are given in the table below:

Mode	Description
r	Activates the reading mode for a file. (normal mode)
w	Prepares a document for editing. If the file does not already exist, it is created.
x	Creates a new file in read-only mode. If the target file already exists, the operation will fail.
a	Retains the original file length when opening a file to append to. If the specified file doesn't already exist, it gets created.
t	A text window will pop up. (default)
b	The binary mode opens.
+	The update file is opened (reading and writing)

Adding the encoding type while opening a file in Python is highly recommended. This will ensure all of the alphabet and the file's contents are preserved.

file = open("doc.txt", mode='w', encoding='utf-8')

Now that our file is opened in writing mode let's add some lines of text.

Writing in a file:

Writing in the file using Python is super simple. We can use the **write()** method. We must be careful what mode we are in **w** mode overwrites existing data, and **a** (append) mode changes add to the same file. A demonstration of the write method is given below:

```
f = open('doc.txt', 'w', encoding='utf-8')

f.write("Hello World! in a text file\n")        # \n is the new line character

f.write("Python\n")
```

Output:

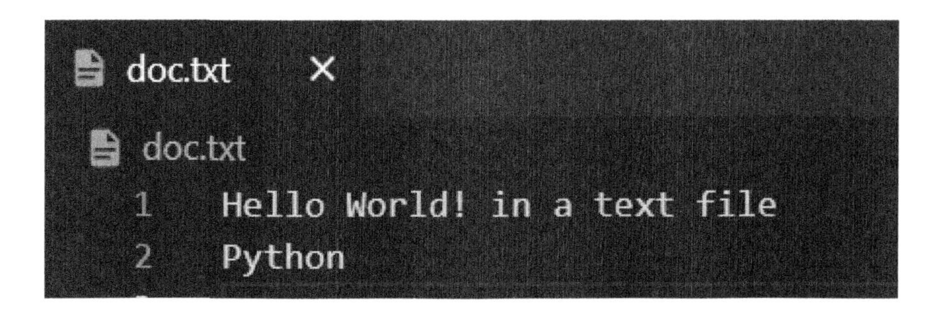

(The output is in the doc.txt file)

Reading a file:

Now that there is data in our text file let's read the contents using Python. This time, open the while using the read mode and **read()** mode.

```
f = open('doc.txt', 'r', encoding='utf-8')

print(f.read())
```

Output:

This will show the contents of the file in the output console:

Hello World! in a text file

Python

Closing a file:

When you are done with file manipulation, you can use the **close()** method to close the file.

```
f = open("doc.txt", encoding = 'utf-8')

f.close()
```

Chapter 14: Objects and Classes in Python

14.1: What is OOP?

OOP stands for **object-oriented programming, popular for writing code and making** abstractions and logic. The basic concept of OOP involves two major terms:

1. Classes
2. Objects

In this chapter, we will look at them both and see how programmers can use OOP to their advantage, and in the upcoming chapter, we will build on the foundation of objects and classes and explore two major concepts regarding OOP.

14.2: What are Classes?

Think about classes like blueprints, which include functions and data that resonate with that class. The structure of defining a class in Python is given below:

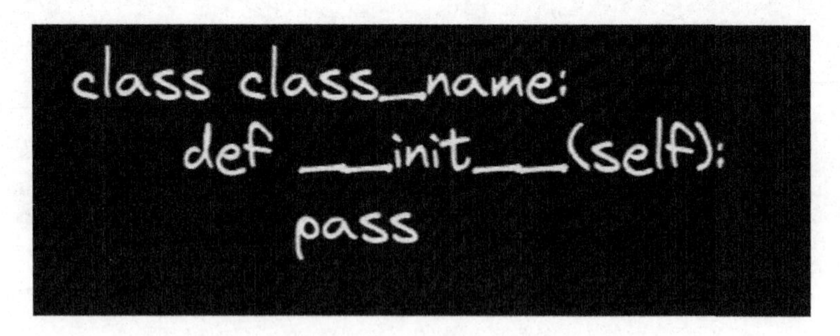

The **class** keyword defines a class (similar to **def** for a function). The next thing is the **init** method, similar to constructors of a class in many other languages like C++. When an instance of the class is created (or an object is created, same thing), the init method is automatically invoked and sets up the object ready for calling other methods.

The **self** parameter is used to represent the class instance. Python's class attributes and methods are made available via this keyword. This connects the specified attributes to the arguments. Let's take a look at a code example of the Animal class:

```
class Animal:
    def __init__(self, name, color):
        self.name = name
        self.color = color
    def print_details(self):
        print(self.name)
        print(self.color)
```

The Animal Class contains two variables: name, color, and a method to print these details. Before we call the method, let's understand objects in Python.

14.3: What are Objects?

Objects show the characteristics and behaviors associated with their classes because they are elements (instances) of those classes. The class defines how instances are created and behave, but the object is the actual component of the program. The structure of defining an object from a class called my_class is like this:

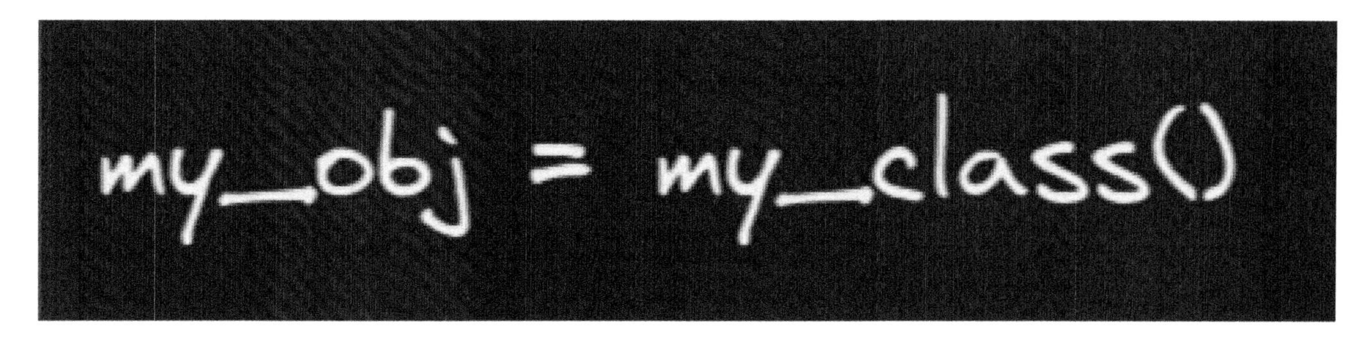

Now using the **dot (.)** operator, we can call the methods defined inside my_class. Let's continue the Animal class example and create a "cat" object

```
# class
class Animal:
  def __init__(self, name, color, type):
    self.name = name
    self.color = color
    self.type = type
  def print_details(self):
    print(self.name)
    print(self.color)
    print(self.type)
# creating an object (class instance):
cat = Animal('Blizzard', 'white', 'cat')
# let's print the detail of this cat:
cat.print_details()
```

Output:

```
Blizzard
white
cat
```

But what if you wanted to create another animal using the same class? This is super simple. All you have to do is create another object.

```
# creating an object (class instance):
cat = Animal('Blizzard', 'white', 'cat')
# let's print the detail of this cat:
cat.print_details()
print('-----')
# another object but this time for a dog:
dog = Animal('Charlie', 'brown', 'dog')
dog.print_details()
```

Output:

```
Blizzard
white
cat
-----
Charlie
brown
dog
```

This clearly shows us that using objects and classes is a clean way to organize and reuse code, but this setup has some open-ended corners. The major issue is that when an object is created, we can access the methods we want to access and other information. Like in the above example, we can access all of the variables while the object was created:

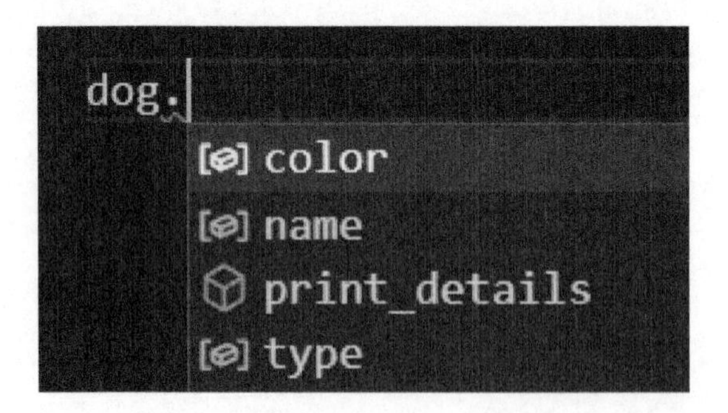

(visual studio code was used for this section of the book, but any IDE can be used)

To solve this issue and restrict the level of access, we have the concept of encapsulation.

14.4: What is encapsulation?

Python's OOP allows us to implement secure access control over our methods and variables. Encapsulation refers to the process of protecting information from unauthorized or direct modification in this way.

In Python, we denote private attributes using a single or double underscore as the prefix. Let's change the **Animal** class and make some attributes private.

```
# class
class Animal:
  def __init__(self, name, color, type):
    self.name = name
    self._color = color
    self.type = type
  def print_details(self):
    print("-----")
    print(self.name)
    print(self._color)
    print(self.type)
    print("-----")
# creating an object (class instance):
dog = Animal("Charlie", "Brown", "dog")    #
initial information
dog.print_details()
# Lets change the color of the dog by
directly accessing the variable:
dog.__color = 'Liver Brown'
dog.print_details()           # printing again
to see changes
```

Now the **color** is a private variable. There is no direct way we can change the color. The output of the code above is:

Output:

~~~~~

Charlie

Brown

dog

~~~~~

~~~~~

Charlie

Brown

dog

~~~~~

As you can see, the dog's color is still just brown even though we tried to change it directly. Now you may ask, what if we needed to change the color? The easiest and safest way is to create a helper function (mostly, programmers only create one getter and one setter method or function, the setter method is there to set the details, and the getter method gets the details like our print_details function). Lets create a **set color()** method

Chapter 15: Inheritance and Polymorphism

15.1: What is Inheritance?

Inheritance is a concept or a feature of OOP (object-oriented programming). Inheritance in English means receiving something from your ancestors, and object-oriented programming also means the same thing.

Inheritance in OOP refers to a new class (child or derived class) which includes its own attributes and information, and it also inherits (or receives) the information of another class (this class is known as base class or parent class). In Python, the general syntax for inheritance is:

In code

```
class Parent():
    def __init__(self):
        pass
class Child(Parent):
    def __init__(self):
```

Let's look at some real-life examples of inheritance: cars and bikes are vehicles (we are generalizing the class here). In programming, this will look like the car class is derived from the class of the vehicle. Let's continue our example of the Animal class and create another class called Birds which is derived from the Animal class:

```
# class
from xmlrpc.client import FastParser
class Animal:
  def __init__(self, name, color, runs):
    self.name = name
    self._color = color
    self.runs = runs
  def set_color(self, color):
    self._color = color;
  def print_details(self):
    print("-----")
    print(self.name)
    print(self._color)
    if self.runs:
      print('runs')
    else:
      print('Does not Run!')
    print("-----")
class Bird(Animal):
  def __init__(self, name, color, runs):
    Animal.__init__(self, name, color, runs)
    self.fly = runs
B = Bird('Hawk', 'black', False)
B.print_details()
```

Output:

```
-----

Hawk

black

Does not Run!

-----
```

Now that we know the basics of inheritance, we can derive classes from multiple classes, which means multilevel inheritance:

15.2: What is Multilevel Inheritance?

A new class derived from multiple classes is called multilevel inheritance. With multiple inheritances, a derived class takes on characteristics from each of its base classes. Multiple inheritances follow the same syntax as single inheritance. Code example:

```
class A:
    pass
class B:
    pass
class C(A, B):
    pass
```

The **C** class here is derived from 2 classes, A and B. The structure is like so for the above example:

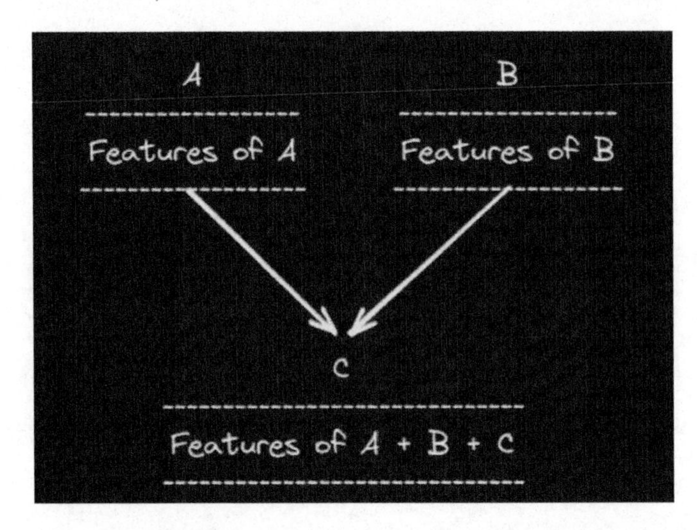

Another way of multilevel inheritance could be:

```
class A:
    pass
class B(A):
    pass
class C(B):
    pass
```

This code kind shows the relation of **grandparent > parent > children**. As the code changes, the inheritance also changes:

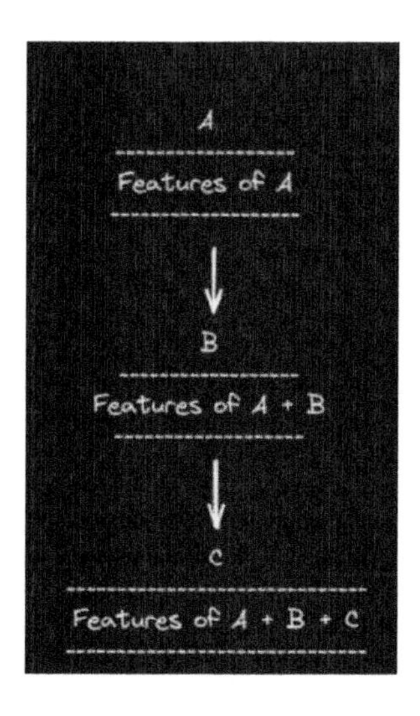

This is all about multilevel inheritance. The next topic is polymorphism in programming.

15.3: Polymorphism in Python

The term "polymorphism" comes from the Greek for "many shapes."

Polymorphism is a very significant concept with plenty of use cases in programming. It denotes employing a single or one type entity (object, method, or operator) to represent many types in several distinct circumstances. In this section, we will look at basic polymorphism on an operator and then apply the same concept to classes. Let's take a look at an example of built-in polymorphism:

How the addition operator is polymorphic:

We recognize that the plus symbol is used to add numbers in Python, such as:

```
x = 3

y = 7

z = x + y

print(z)
```

This will give us an output of 10, and similarly, we can add floating numbers with the same + symbol, but the question raises when we are doing the same operation with a different type of data type, such as **strings.** When we add two strings, the concatenation of strings happens using the same addition symbol:

```
x = 'Hel'

y = 'lo'

z = x + y

print(z)
```

Output:

Hello

This is known as operator overloading or operator polymorphism, and When it comes to Python polymorphism, this example is the simplest. You are probably wondering if we can overload operators. Can we overload custom operations? The answer to that question is yes! Let's now take a look at function polymorphism. For this example, we are going to use the famous **len()** function,

We know that the len() function returns the length for strings:

```
print(len('wow a very long string!'))
```

The above code will print 23, which is the length of "wow a very long string!". Now similarly, we can find the number of items inside the list or a dictionary using the same function (*len*), and it works the same for example, a list containing 6 elements:

```
my_list = [1,2,3,4,5,6]

print(len(my_list))
```

This will print **6**, and the point is the len function in Python is polymorphic as it can run on various data types. Still, it provides different or specific information regarding that data type. In the case of strings, the len function returned the total length of that string; in the case of a dictionary, it returned the number of items inside the list.

15.4 Polymorphism in Classes

Python's child classes can take on the functionality of their parent classes through the inheritance of both methods and attributes. By using a technique called "Method Overriding," we can tailor the implementation of a given set of methods and properties to a subclass.

Because of polymorphism, we can use the same names for both the parent class's original methods and attributes and the overridden versions.from math import pi as PI

class Shape:

```
def __init__(self, shape_name):
    self.n = shape_name
  def cal_area(self):
    pass
  def print_fact(self):
    return "I'm a 2D shape."
  def __name__(self):
    return self.n
class MySquare(Shape):
  def __init__(self, length):
```

As you can see, redefining a function that is already in the parent class will override it only for that class **(in our case, the fact() and area()).**In the above code, the fact is overridden because of polymorphism, so it prints the fact of the square class, not the parent **Shapes** class, and in a circle, it prints the **fact** from the parent class, and there is no redefinition of **fact()** in the **circle** class.

```
super().__init__("Square")
    self.l = length
  def cal_area(self):
    return self.l ** 2
  def print_fact(self):
    return "All the angles in a square are the same, at ninety (90)
degrees."
class MyCircle(Shape):
  def __init__(self, radius):
    super().__init__("Circle")
    self.r = radius
  def cal_area(self):
    return PI * self.r ** 2
s = MySquare(4)
c = MyCircle(10)
print(s.__name__())
print(s.print_fact())
print("---------")
print(c.__name__())
print(c.print_fact())
print(c.cal_area())
```

Output:

```
Square
All the angles in a square are the same, at ninety (90) degrees.
---------
Circle
I'm a 2D shape.
314.1592653589793
```

Conclusion

Now that we've reached this point, the book is now over. We are grateful that you have taken the time to read this book, and we hope you have liked it. Most significantly, it is our earnest goal that the book has assisted you in developing a strong foundational understanding of Python programming as soon as you begin putting everything you have learned into practice. Try the activities and the challenges by yourself as much as you can. The more you do, the more you'll understand. In this book, you have been familiarized with the basics of the python programming language, and you must be able to download it and work with it. The first section of this book dealt with getting to know Python in very layman's terms; in the second chapter, everything to download and run Python in your windows, macOS, and Linux operating systems were discussed. Fast forward to the next chapters, we have discussed some built-in features, such as Data Types, Variables, IDLE, and Python shell and Operators, etc. This book can serve as either an introductory manual for students just learning Python or a reference for experienced Python developers working in the business world.

This book is ideal if you are new to programming in Python 3 or if you need to update code written in Python 2. This one-of-a-kind book is perfect for students just starting with Python and interested in learning about the latest and greatest programming frameworks and idioms. All examples were developed and tested with Python 3.10.6.

Printed in Great Britain
by Amazon